Career Finder

Career Finder

Where to go from here for a successful future

Gill Hasson

CAPSTONE
A Wiley Brand

This edition first published 2021

© 2021 by Gill Hasson

Registered office
John Wiley & Sons Ltd, The Atrium, Southern Gate, Chichester, West Sussex, PO19 8SQ, United Kingdom

For details of our global editorial offices, for customer services and for information about how to apply for permission to reuse the copyright material in this book please see our website at www.wiley.com.

Wiley publishes in a variety of print and electronic formats and by print-on-demand. Some material included with standard print versions of this book may not be included in e-books or in print-on-demand. If this book refers to media such as a CD or DVD that is not included in the version you purchased, you may download this material at http:// booksupport.wiley.com. For more information about Wiley products, visit www.wiley .com.

Designations used by companies to distinguish their products are often claimed as trademarks. All brand names and product names used in this book are trade names, service marks, trademarks or registered trademarks of their respective owners. The publisher is not associated with any product or vendor mentioned in this book.

Limit of Liability/Disclaimer of Warranty: While the publisher and author have used their best efforts in preparing this book, they make no representations or warranties with respect to the accuracy or completeness of the contents of this book and specifically disclaim any implied warranties of merchantability or fitness for a particular purpose. It is sold on the understanding that the publisher is not engaged in rendering professional services and neither the publisher nor the author shall be liable for damages arising herefrom. If professional advice or other expert assistance is required, the services of a competent professional should be sought.

Library of Congress Cataloging-in-Publication Data

Names: Hasson, Gill, author.
Title: Career finder : where to go from here for a successful future / Gill Hasson.
Description: Chichester, West Sussex, United Kingdom : Wiley-Capstone, 2021. | Includes index.
Identifiers: LCCN 2020043581 (print) | LCCN 2020043582 (ebook) | ISBN 9780857088642 (paperback) | ISBN 9780857088659 (adobe pdf) | ISBN 9780857088604 (epub)
Subjects: LCSH: Vocational guidance.
Classification: LCC HF5381 .H287 2021 (print) | LCC HF5381 (ebook) | DDC 650.1—dc23
LC record available at https://lccn.loc.gov/2020043581
LC ebook record available at https://lccn.loc.gov/2020043582

Cover Design: Wiley
Cover Image: © kathayut kongmanee/Shutterstock

Set in 12/15pt, SabonLTStd by SPi Gobal, Chennai, India
Printed and bound by CPI Group (UK) Ltd, Croydon, CR0 4YY

10 9 8 7 6 5 4 3 2 1

Contents

Introduction

Find out what you like doing best and get someone to pay you for doing it.

Katherine Whitehorn

Why do people end up working in jobs and careers they don't like? It's not that they're bad jobs; they could be jobs other people *do* like doing. In general, people end up in jobs or careers they don't like for one or more of the following reasons:

- Their job or career doesn't reflect who they really are: there's a mismatch between their values, interests, strengths, skills, and abilities and the job they're doing or the career they're in.
- They aren't aware of the huge range of jobs and careers that are out there, that are available to them, and would be a good fit for them.
- Once they have identified a job or career they'd like to do, they don't know what opportunities to pursue to maximize their chances of getting an 'in'.

You don't have to be one of these people!

Identifying the work and career that's right for you – that you'll like and enjoy doing, is a process of discovery and learning.

Not only do you need to find out more about yourself and the jobs and careers that are available, you also need to know that, whatever path you decide to follow, it doesn't have to be fixed. These days, careers are dynamic; they're characterized by changing world events, changing personal circumstances, new ideas and directions. Chapter 1 starts by explaining this. It describes how each of us has to take responsibility for managing the nature, direction, and development of our own career. And that's a good thing! It means that you get to define and create your own working life: you become the author of your career.

Chapters 2 and 3 help you to learn more about yourself – to identify your values and interests; your skills, strengths, and qualities; and your own preferred way of learning and doing things. Having done that, you'll then have a clearer idea of who you are. You'll know what your values are: the importance, for you, of what you put into and get out of your work. You'll have identified your attributes – your strengths – and your skills – what you're good at doing. You'll also have identified the way that you naturally approach learning and doing things.

Next, you can start to explore what jobs and careers there are and think about how they might be of interest and be a good fit for you. Chapter 4 discusses whether or not there's a perfect job out there for you. You may be hoping that once you've found your passion everything else will fall into place. But what if you don't have a passion or a 'calling'? There's little or nothing you feel particularly enthusiastic about or inspired to do? No problem!

You don't *have* to have a calling, a big idea or a long-term career plan. Instead, you identify what *might* be of interest and be a good direction, do some research, and learn from what you find out along the way. Chapter 4 helps you discover the wide range of jobs and careers out there and explains how to narrow them down to a few that are most of interest to you.

Once you've identified some possible jobs and careers, as well as the criteria to judge them by – the extent to which they match your interests, values, skills, and strengths – the next step is to find out about them in more detail. Chapter 5 explains a number of ways you can do this.

Once you've narrowed down your ideas and options you'll want to know what opportunities you could pursue to maximize your chances of getting into the job, profession, or career that interests you. In Chapter 6 you can read about internships and work placements, returnships and apprenticeships.

In Chapters 4, 5, and 6 there are details about many of the organizations that can give you further advice and guidance. The section at the back of the book – Websites and further information – also has contact details for organizations that provide information about internships, apprenticeships, voluntary work, writing CVs, application forms, etc.

Chapter 7 explains what a portfolio career is and how it could work for you. This chapter is particularly useful if you're thinking about making a career change.

Chapter 8 moves on to what to do if you are currently stuck in a job or career you don't like but, for whatever reason, you're unable to leave for now. There's plenty of positive advice if you're in that position right now. There's also advice and support around what to do if you actually hate your job or a course of study you've embarked on. And finally, there's constructive advice about managing unemployment.

Whether you're stuck in a job you don't like or you're unemployed, whether you're still in education or just leaving it, or you're thinking about a career change, the emphasis throughout this book is that your attitude and approach make all the difference. You'll need a positive mindset, persistence, and determination. You'll also need an open mind; a willingness to be adaptable and flexible.

Finding the right job and career for you might not be easy, but if you follow the steps described in this book, you'll not only ensure that you're heading in the right direction, but you'll do so with enthusiasm and confidence.

1
The Changing Nature of Careers

The pen that writes your life story must be held in your own hand.

Irene C. Kassorla

What *is* a career? Like most people, you probably think of a career as the work a person does throughout their working life, in a specific profession or industry. We talk about a 'career path' and a 'career ladder'; we see a career as something we make progress in, with opportunities for promotion, an increase in responsibilities and pay, and other benefits.

Although we're all familiar with the concept of a career, it is, in fact, a relatively recent concept.

In the past, most people simply did the work that was there; they did what their circumstances and environment presented them with. If, say, you lived in an agricultural community, your work was in agriculture, working on a farm or in associated work; as a blacksmith, for example. If you lived in a fishing community your work

3

was in the fishing industry and if you lived in a mining community, you worked in or at the surface of the mines. In the towns and cities, you might have worked in a trade; you might, for example, have been a draper, or a goldsmith, a tailor, a cordwainer, a plasterer, or a bookbinder. Whether a person lived in a town or a city, as a rule, if their family did it, so did they.

In the middle of the nineteenth century, the advent of the Industrial Revolution brought people work in the factories and work with large employers, such as railway companies.

By the twentieth century, and throughout the following decades, access to an education widened the possibility for many individuals to enter a profession and build a career. Typically, people secured a job after leaving school, college, or university and they either stayed there or moved on to maybe one or two other employers during their working life. Employees were loyal towards the company or organization they worked for, and were confident of a high level of job security. Within the organization, there was a clear line of promotion; employees aimed to work their way up the career ladder in order to gain promotion and the associated benefits: increased responsibilities, pay, status, and a decent pension at the end.

The organization you worked for mapped out your career; they provided career opportunities and progress. Now, though, many of the organizations and companies that used to offer steady lifelong jobs are no longer presenting a linear career path and/or the security that previous generations experienced.

> The three-stage life of education, work and retirement is clearly not fit for purpose. That's a huge shift for the young as they consider lifetime learning and multiple career shifts. What worked for their grandparents' generation won't work for them. And it's not only the young who face this challenge – those in their forties and fifties have to plan for longer careers in a world where jobs will be changing with technology and their skills may no longer be relevant.
>
> Lynda Gratton – professor of management practice and Andrew J Scott, professor of economics, both at London Business School.

Professors Gratton and Scott, authors of the book, *The New Long Life: A Framework for Flourishing in a Changing World*, suggest that 'a core aspect of this new multi stage life is that it is "self-authored", in the sense that the dynamics and trajectory lie with you, rather than, as was the case in the past, with your employer. When we live longer, we inevitably have more transitions – from one job to another, but also from a job to a time to learn, or from a job to a time to care.'

Today, even if you do stay in one profession or industry or with one employer, you might travel a career path that changes direction. The UK's Civil Service, for example, on their career page https://civil-service-careers.gov.uk/ suggests to prospective employees that 'whatever your passion, to specialize or try something new, there's a path for you.'

From A&E nurse to psychotherapist

In 1995, at the age of 31, Donna Butler started work as a staff nurse in the A&E department of Brighton's Royal Sussex County Hospital. She soon became aware of the stressful impact – whether in a cumulative way or from single traumatic incidents – that working in A&E was having on her and her colleagues. Too often, staff struggled to cope with the stress: they either carried on and their mental health suffered – depression and anxiety and/or trauma and burnout – or they left the job.

Donna identified a clear need and determined to do something to support herself and her colleagues. She took the initiative and, for the next four years, while continuing to work in A&E, she studied for a counselling degree so that she could qualify and register as a psychotherapist with the aim of persuading the hospital to give her a post supporting her colleagues in A&E.

After qualifying in counselling in 2002, Donna devised a questionnaire asking all staff in different departments at the hospital if they felt they would be better supported in their jobs if they had access to counselling therapy: 98% said yes. As a result, the hospital agreed to create a new post for Donna as a counsellor offering a safe, confidential place to talk, supporting A&E staff, patients, and relatives with counselling and to facilitate debriefs following specific traumatic events on the unit.

In 2009, after eight years of delivering the counselling service in A&E, Donna determined to widen both her knowledge (she studied for and achieved a master's in Integrated Psychotherapy) and the counselling service she was providing.

She presented the executive team and hospital board with a business plan to make a counselling, psychotherapy, and training service available as an 'in-house' provision to all Brighton and Sussex University Hospitals NHS Trust's 9,000 staff.

Donna is now the lead psychotherapist with a team of therapists – delivering the Trust's Health, Employee, Learning and Psychotherapy service. She also became part of the senior HR team and leads on advising the Trust on psychological care for staff.

So, while some people may stay with the same organization, and move up the career ladder in the conventional way, some, like Donna, stay with the same organization but move into a very different role.

Then there are other people who can't or don't want to rely on one organization to provide the structure and opportunities around which they can develop a career. Instead, they move to a different employer every few years in order to progress. In fact, according to recent research by life insurance firm LV=, on average, a UK worker will change employer every five years.

Increasingly, people change professions completely. One person I know has gone from being a plumber in his 20s to becoming a fire officer in the Fire and Rescue Service in his 30s. One friend went from working in book design for 30 years to working as a tree surgeon. Another friend changed direction from being an illustrator to becoming a portrait painter. Someone else I know went from working in hospitality to working in social media. And one friend, who I met when we were both waitressing as teenagers, many years ago, went on to be a pop star, then a TV producer and an investigative journalist, and is now a furniture maker.

Writing in the *Financial Times* in September 2017, Work and Careers Editor Helen Barrett described having recently met a woman in her fifties who was soon to qualify as a lawyer, her fourth career.

Helen explained that for this woman, an early academic career had led to museum work, and, by her thirties, she was curating exhibitions at leading international galleries in London and Berlin. 'In her forties,' Helen wrote, 'she developed a sideline: teaching the practicalities of entrepreneurship to art undergraduates. This turned into a fascination with intellectual property law. At 46, she started legal training. Years later, she is now a trainee for a boutique intellectual property law firm in the City of London. In another year or so she will be qualified. Would it be her last career? She couldn't say.'

Some people spend their working life with one employer, others change employers and change professions every few years. Many people eschew being employed by someone else and set up their own business, work freelance, and are self-employed. And some people have more than one career at the same time – a portfolio career: a portfolio of jobs which involves dividing their time and skills between two or more part-time jobs, one or more of which may be self-employed.

Clearly, then, career paths are far less predictable than they once were. There's been a huge shift from individuals relying on their employer for job security and career development to individuals taking responsibility for their own career management and employability.

Over a person's lifetime, their own personal circumstances – their values, skills, abilities, and interests – change. There are continual economic and technological changes at local, national, and global level; economies collapse, companies go under, entire professions get automated by technology. And pandemics occur. All of which impact on each and every one of us in terms of jobs, work, and a career.

In good times and bad, whether life appears to be stable and secure or uncertain and unclear, we must manage our own work and career and create our own opportunities. We each need to be open to new ways of thinking and doing and be willing to acquire new knowledge and skills.

Career progress or 'success' is no longer measured by how far up an organization's hierarchy a person can climb. Career success and progress is now more subjective: a 'good job', 'good work', and a 'successful career' is defined by you, the individual; it's work that is consistent with your own personal values, circumstances, and priorities at any one period of your life.

What career success means is down to you; you can have your own definition of success and use this definition to guide you in your career choices.

Rather than see a career as a ladder to be climbed, it's more appropriate and helpful to liken a career to a road trip. In the past, a career was like getting on a bus or a train; there was a clearly defined route with stop-off points and a clear destination. Now, the direction and progress in a career is more within your control and your responsibility. As with any road trip, you control your departure and arrival time, the directions, the itinerary, and stops along the way. Delays – road works, bad weather, diversions, breakdown, or accidents – have to be taken into account and managed. You may have a plan – a map – but you don't have to follow it. You might come across something of interest and take a break to have a look. You could find something of interest you'd like to spend longer at or spot something in the distance that prompts you to take a new direction. You are the one in the driving seat!

Is it Possible to Find Work and a Career that You Enjoy and Are Happy With?

> How we spend our days is, of course, how we spend our lives.
>
> Annie Dillard

For many of us, work fills a large part of our lives; the average person spends a quarter of their adult life at work; it's reckoned that we will spend 3,507 days at work over a lifetime.

In her book *How to have a Happy Hustle* Bec Evans writes: 'At school when asked what I wanted to be when I grew up, I replied that I wanted to be happy. Not a helpful response for my teacher who was trying to organise my Year 10 work placement.'

Is it realistic to think that you can find work and a career that you enjoy and are happy with? To answer this, it helps to understand what makes for happiness and fulfilment. Over 2,000 years ago, the Greek philosopher Aristotle identified two types of happiness: hedonic happiness and eudaimonic happiness. Hedonic happiness is the small pleasures and eudaimonic happiness refers to happiness that comes from having meaning, purpose, and fulfilment in our lives.

Aristotle suggested that because, as human beings, we have a unique ability think, to rationalize and reason, to make judgements, and come to conclusions, we should – indeed we *must* – use this ability to work out for ourselves ways to live our lives so that we have a sense of purpose and meaning and that we experience a general, stable sense of well-being, feel fulfilled and believe that, overall, life is good.

Aristotle acknowledged that, of course, happiness can be affected by external issues – our environment, our health, the actions of other people, etc. – but, he said, by using our ability to think and reason, we are able to create a life for ourselves that enables us to bear the ups and downs with balance and perspective and maintain a general sense of well-being.

Fast forward 2,000 years and, like Aristotle, today's psychologists and researchers are also interested in what makes for happiness and a good life. Positive Psychology Professor, Martin Seligman, for example, in his book *Flourish*, also suggests that in order to be happy, as well as small pleasures, connecting with others, and feeling that we belong, we need to have one or more things in our life that mean something and make sense to us, that interest and absorb us, that we want to be involved in and allow us to feel good when we achieve what we set out to do.

Of course, what is meaningful, engaging, and gives a sense of purpose is different for everyone. But for so many of us, because work is such a key part of our lives, it's our work that can provide meaning, engagement, and a sense of purpose. Or, to look at it another way; it's *because* much of our time is spent at work that it *needs* to be meaningful, engage us, and provide a sense of purpose.

What's Getting in the Way?

So, if a job, work, or career can provide meaning and purpose and can help us feel fulfilled, why don't we all just go get ourselves a brilliant, meaningful, purpose-filled job, work, or career?

There are a range of reasons. Does one or more of these reasons sound like you?

- I have no idea what I want to do. (But I feel that I should!)
- There's nothing that really interests, inspires, or enthuses me.
- I have a job or a career, but it's going nowhere. I feel there are few, if any, options.
- There's more than one option. I can't decide; I'm going round in circles.
- I have something in mind but I'm worried I might pursue it then not like it.
- I know what I want to do but it will take years of study before I'd qualify and be able to earn a living.
- I have a passion I want to turn into a career but I don't know how to go about it.
- I know what I want to do but don't know how to get an 'in'.
- I know what I'd like to do but I'm not clever enough/I'm too old, it's too late/it won't pay enough/I'd have to move/I have physical or mental health difficulties/I have caring responsibilities for family members/there may not be opportunities for career progress.
- I can't see the bigger picture; what might the future hold? What might I need to think about re future opportunities or problems – technology, world events, etc?

- I feel pressured and confused by family, friends, or colleagues who are telling me to follow a particular job or career: 'Choose this career; it pays well and/or will give you status.' 'Choose the safe path.' 'A job is just a job. Work isn't meant to be fulfilling.' 'So-and-so loves her job, you should do that too.' Or, 'So-and-so hates his job, don't ever do what he's doing.'

Not knowing what to do or how to go about it, or whether it will be the right choice, whether you'll be good enough, how you can do it with the commitments and responsibilities you have, etc. are all valid concerns.

But, the good news is that those concerns all come with solutions. And they're all in this book!

You *don't* have to know what you want to do and have one vocation for the rest of your working life. You might not have an idea of exactly what your career path looks like and that's OK. Yes, it's helpful to think where you'd like to be in two three, five, or 10 years' time, but also know that things can change; even if you did know what you wanted to do, you'd still probably change because of world events, technology etc. Your future job might not even exist yet! Whatever you do next or plan to do in the near future, you might change your mind after five, 10, 20, or even 30 years; it's likely you'll have several different paths or one path that will go off in different directions.

Instead of long-term career plans, think along the lines of short-term career plans: two to five years. Think in terms of a range of possibilities and opportunities that could come up at some point down the line. Think in terms of developing your knowledge, skills, and experience.

Perhaps you feel that there's nothing that interests or enthuses you enough to make a career out of. You don't need to start with a brilliant idea or burning passion; you just need to make a start with something and move forward from there. There's a wealth of ideas and information about a huge range of jobs and careers out there.

Perhaps you *do* have a passion: a burning interest that you want to turn into a career but you don't know how to go about it or you know what you want to do but don't know how to get an 'in'. No problem! There's plenty of advice and information out there; you just have to do some research. Chapter 5 explains this.

Maybe, though, you're interested in more than one line of work or one specific career; there's more than one option, you can't decide, you're going round in circles. Not to worry; it's not so difficult to narrow it down – knowing your values, skills, and abilities can help; the next two chapters explain how. It's also possible that you won't have to make a choice – it's possible to follow more than one interest in an area of work/profession; to have a portfolio career. Chapter 7 explains how you can do this.

It could be that you have something in mind but you're concerned that you might pursue it then realize you don't like it. That's OK – there's no need to commit to something before you're absolutely sure; there are a number of ways you can find out about a potential line of work, profession, or career before you commit to it. And even if at some point you change your mind, it's not as difficult as you might think, to change direction. You simply need to take a path that feels right today and know that you can re-evaluate in the future; change what you do or the direction you take as and when circumstances present themselves – opportunities, challenges, setbacks, etc.

Maybe you know what you want to do but you're concerned that it will take years of training and study before you'd qualify and be able to earn a living. Certainly, that's true for some professions, but for so many other jobs and professions, there's often more than one path; apprenticeships, for example, allow you to earn while you learn. You can find out more about apprenticeships in Chapter 6.

What if you know what you'd like to do but you believe you can't do it because you're not clever enough/you're too old, it's too late? Perhaps you believe that what you'd really like to do won't pay enough or you'd have to move to a different part of the country? Or you might have physical or mental health difficulties or else you have caring responsibilities for family members and think that would exclude you from pursuing a particular career. Maybe you believe that the career that interests you might not offer much in the way of opportunities for career progress? The answer to all these concerns is to recognize that they are assumptions; beliefs for which you may not have any concrete evidence. Again – there's a wide range of advice and information available that can help you navigate your way to the work you'd like to do.

Finally, what to do about the career advice and pressure from family and friends? Whether you told them you were planning on training to be a horse whisperer, a microbiologist or tarot card reader, a brain surgeon or a florist, there's always going to be someone who thinks you're doing it all wrong. Listen instead to Dave Grohl, the front man of the Foo Fighters, who said 'No one is you and that is your power.'

Steve Jobs, co-founder of Apple, had some good advice too, he said: 'Your time is limited so don't waste it living someone else's life. Don't be trapped by dogma which is living with the results of other people's thinking. Don't let the noise of others' opinions drown out your own inner voice. And most importantly, have the courage to follow your heart and intuition. They somehow already know what you truly want to become.'

The quest to do work you enjoy, that's right for you, is a process of discovery and experimentation. There are three key steps. You need to:

- Know more about yourself; what your values are – what's important to you, what your skills, strengths, and abilities are.
- Know what's out there; what jobs, professions, trades, and careers there are. (There are thousands!)
- Know what you can do to maximize your chances of getting the work or career that appeals to you. This doesn't mean knowing how to fill in a job application form, write a CV, or behave in an interview. There's plenty of information about CVs, application forms etc. online for you to read (see the websites on page 157). Rather, it's about knowing what opportunities you can pursue that will lead to the work and career you're interested in.

Your attitude, not your aptitude, will determine your altitude.

Zig Ziglar

Most importantly, to find what you want to do or to work towards, to have enjoyable fulfilling work, you must be prepared to put time and effort into finding it. You'll need a positive approach – an open mind, to be flexible and willing to try new things. You'll need to manage difficulties and challenges and be solution-focused.

In a nutshell

- Career paths are far less predictable than they once were. There's been a huge shift from people relying on their employer for job security and career development, to people taking responsibility for their own career management and employability.

- Some people do spend their working life with one employer – in the same role or in different roles. Others change employers or change professions every few years. Other people set up their own business, work freelance, and are self-employed. And some people have a portfolio of jobs, dividing their time and skills between two or more part-time jobs, one or more of which may be self-employed.

- In order to enjoy your work and to feel fulfilled, it needs to be meaningful, engage you, and provide a sense of purpose. What's meaningful and makes for career success is down to each of us as individuals: you must create your own definition of success and use this definition to guide you in your career choices.

- Whatever your circumstances, and whatever's happening in the world, you'll need a positive approach; to be flexible and able to adapt, open to new ways of thinking and doing. You'll need to be willing to acquire new knowledge and skills.

- There's a range of issues and difficulties – all valid – that can get in the way of getting yourself a brilliant, meaningful, purpose-filled job, work, or career. Fortunately, those difficulties all come with solutions!
- The quest to do work that's right for you is a process of discovery and experimentation. You need to find out more about yourself and you'll need to research a number of jobs, professions, and careers. You must also take advantage of the opportunities that will maximize your chances of getting into the work or career that's right for you.

2
Knowing Who You Are and What's Important to You

I hope that what you're going through right now can be your wake-up call, that it pushes you not just to think about what kind of career you want to build, but what kind of person you want to be.

Michelle Obama

In the last chapter you will have read that being happy and feeling fulfilled in your work or career involves being engaged in work that is meaningful and provides a sense of purpose; that engages you in a way that means something and makes sense to you, that interests and absorbs you, that allows you to achieve in some way and to feel good about what you've achieved.

But what is meaningful, engaging, and gives a sense of purpose is different for everyone. So how do you find out what that might be for you? You start by identifying your values.

We all have values and we each have different values. Maybe you've not given much thought to what your values are, but that doesn't mean you don't have them. Quite simply, your values are what's important to you and has some worth to you in the way that you live, work, and relate to other people.

No doubt you'll have heard the exhortation to 'Just be true to yourself!' and may have wondered what exactly that means; how do you be 'true' to yourself? Well, when you're living your life and working in ways that are in line with your values, when you're doing what's important to you – not what you think you 'should' be doing or what other people think is important – then you're being true to yourself. You're being real, genuine, and authentic. Admittedly, being true to yourself isn't always the easy path – there are challenges and difficulties – but ultimately, you'll be living your life in a way that reflects who and what you really are and want to be.

The first thing that stops many people from living a life that's true to them is the fact that they haven't actually identified *what* is true to them; they haven't clarified what their values are; what's meaningful and important to them. So, identifying your values is the first step.

What have your values got to do with being in the 'right' job, doing the 'right' work or career?

If you're working in a job that *doesn't* match your values much of the time, you could feel like an impostor; you're not being who you really are. But when your work matches your values, things will just feel right; your work and career will feel compatible with who you are and what's important to you. And that will help you to feel you're doing work that has meaning and purpose for you; work that makes sense and that you have your own good reasons to do.

Your values become your destiny.

Mahatma Gandhi

Identify Your Values

What do you value? To help you identify your values, here is a list of some common core values. Tick any that are important to you. Add any you think of that aren't included on the list.

Achievement
Adventure
Affection
Altruism
Ambition
Amusement
Appreciation
Approachability
Approval
Balance
Beauty
Belonging
Calmness
Care
Certainty

Courtesy
Creativity
Curiosity
Decisiveness
Dependability
Determination
Dignity
Directness
Discipline
Discretion
Duty
Empathy
Enjoyment
Equality
Excellence

Clarity
Commitment
Compassion
Confidence
Connection
Consistency
Continuity
Contributing
Control
Cooperation
Courage
Humility
Independence
Integrity
Intimacy
Justice
Kindness
Loyalty
Open-mindedness
Optimism
Peace
Perfection
Persistence
Popularity
Privacy
Professionalism
Punctuality
Reliability

Excitement
Fairness
Family
Fidelity
Freedom of speech
Frugality
Fun
Generosity
Gratitude
Harmony
Honesty
Respect
Security
Self-control
Self-reliance
Simplicity
Sincerity
Spirituality
Spontaneity
Stability
Structure
Success
Support
Trust
Truth
Understanding
Unity

Identify Your Core, Intrinsic Values

Once you've been through the list, narrow it down to between five and seven values. Write them down. These are your 'core' values; your most important, essential values. They are intrinsic – they are a key aspect of who you truly are.

Some of your values are likely to be personal values; values that are concerned with how you behave and respond to situations; values such as optimism, clarity, determination, or security. You will probably also have social values – values such as compassion, fairness and cooperation, reliability or honesty – which concern the way you interact with other people. You may have more personal values than social values. You may have more social values than personal values. It doesn't matter – whatever your values, they are what are important to *you*.

Interpret and Better Understand Your Core Values

Now give some thought to what each of those core values means to you. Different values mean different things to different people so it's useful to define what each value means to you and how it relates to your life.

You might find it helpful to write it down. The process of explaining in writing what each value means to you can help you further clarify what and why it's important to you. For each value, answer these questions:

- What does the word (the value) mean? What does the dictionary say this word means? (Look it up in an online dictionary such as www.dictionary.com) Do I agree with that definition? How would I describe to someone else what this word means to me, how it applies to my life?
- Why is this value important to me?
- In what way is this value currently a part of my life? How do I live this value? If, for example, kindness and compassion were values, how, where, and when am I able to give or receive kindness and compassion? And if stability is a value – it's important to me – in what ways is it present in my life?

Extrinsic Values; Work Values

Your core values are intrinsic values; they are the values you bring to a job, your work, your career. As well as core, intrinsic values, you will also have work values; these are extrinsic values. Extrinsic values are concerned with what you get out of your work, rather than what you put into it.

Examples of extrinsic values include level of earnings, status, and job security. Perhaps job security or promotion opportunities are important to you? Maybe it's having authority, leadership and influence, prestige and high pay. Perhaps flexible hours, low levels of responsibility, being shown appreciation, and a pleasant environment are important to you in a job. Or maybe a job where no two days are the same is important to you – you like to be involved in a variety of tasks and activities. Maybe it's important to you to be involved with work that's practical, creative, or inventive. Or you like to be able to work on your own; to be autonomous and make all your own decisions.

Work Values

How important is each of the following factors in a job? Rate each one on a scale of 1–6, where 6 is 'extremely important for me' and 1 is 'completely unimportant for me'.

I can get ahead and progress in a career	A
I can help people cope better with their lives	Sup
I'm highly paid	E
Job security is guaranteed	Se
I can work independently of others	In
I can do things which involve some risk	R
I can enjoy high social status	P
I am not office-based – I get out and about	V
I like the place/the surroundings where I work	En
I can do work that's socially useful – I can make a difference	Sup
I get to develop new ideas or products	C
There is little work-related stress	Se
People respect me for my position	P

There are opportunities to be promoted	A
There are new challenges and ventures	R
Things are left entirely to my judgement – I get to make the decisions	In
There is a pleasant working environment	En
I am in charge of other people	Au
I can work as part of a team	S
I can be creative or inventive	C
A very good standard of living will be possible	E
There are friendly, supportive people as colleagues	S
There is a lot of variety in what I do	V
I have authority to get things done	Au

Work Values Score Sheet

Add up the scores for each category and identify your top three values.

Advancement	A
Promotion and more responsibility	
Social	S
Working with other people	
Economic	E
Well paid	
Security	Se
Job stability and regular income	
Independence	In
Be able to determine the nature and timing of my work, without too much direction from others	

Variety	V
The work involves a range of tasks and responsibilities	
Position	P
Respect and social status	
Environment	En
Pleasant physical surroundings	
Support	Sup
Helping people. Work of social or community value	
Creative	C
New ideas. Creative solutions to problems	
Risk	R
An element of uncertainty	
Authority	Au
Leading and influencing others. Making decisions	

My Top Three Work Values Are:

What else might be important to you in a job? What other work values might you have? If you've worked in the past, think about what you've liked and enjoyed about each job. And what you've disliked. Flexible hours, the ability to work from home, opportunities to learn and develop your skills and knowledge – are any of these extrinsic/work values important to you? Write them down.

If you currently work, try keeping a 'values diary' for a couple of weeks. At the end of each day, make a note of what you did or what happened at work – the negatives and the positives – and how they do or don't relate to/reflect your values; your core intrinsic values and your extrinsic work values.

Combining core values and work values

Some years ago, in a newspaper interview Anita Roddick, founder of the beauty products company The Body Shop, said: 'I've never been able to separate Body Shop values from my own core values; values of optimism, fun, caring, family and community.' And later, on her website, she wrote, 'It's impossible to separate the company values from the issues that I care passionately about – social responsibility, respect for human rights, the environment and animal protection, and an absolute belief in Community Trade.'

Using your values to help you make decisions about work and a career to pursue means you're less likely to be influenced by what others think you 'ought' to do or 'should' do.

Perhaps the work you do or the career you currently have, or are aiming towards, is more a reflection of what someone else – your teachers, friends, or family – told you was important in a job or career. For example, if your parents held qualifications, status, and high earnings amongst their work values it's more than likely that they impressed those values on you too. But what if you don't share the same values and, actually, you would rather be selling ice cream on a beach in the South of France? Or perhaps you aspire to be a tree surgeon rather than a heart surgeon? You want to be a tattoo artist, not a fine artist?

If, rather than pursuing your own values and doing what you think is important, you're working or aiming for a career according to values that are not yours – that are not a true reflection of who you really are – you might struggle to be happy at work or in a career because you're going in a direction that takes you away from what's important to you; what really makes sense and has meaning to you.

Identifying your core, intrinsic values and your extrinsic values – your work values – is a good first step towards knowing more about what work or career might be a good fit for you. It's not always easy to live and work according to your values; it can involve effort, perseverance, taking some risks, and making sacrifices.

Making a decision based on work values

Mel is an illustrator. 'Two years ago I decided to leave my job as an illustrator for a book publishing company to work freelance. I worried about changing from a secure income to an uncertain one but my work values had shifted – it had become important to me to have more flexible hours, more control over my days and pursue the type of illustrative work I was really interested in and liked doing.

The first year wasn't easy. Pitching for work, waiting to hear if I'd been successful and chasing invoices are the two things I really didn't like about working freelance. I also had to get used to the change from working with five or six other people in a studio to just me on my own working in my flat.

Despite that, I'm happier! I've got the flexibility and control I was aiming for and I adapted to the changes and learnt to manage the challenges; I'm building up a list of clients who give me work and I've stopped spending so much time and energy getting het up about potential clients that don't get back to me. I've dropped them. And I've saved up an emergency fund so that I can cover my bills when clients don't pay on time.'

Every now and again you'll need to review your values: your intrinsic core values and your extrinsic work values. Your life and circumstances will of course go through changes. What's important to you now might not be the same in the future. Be aware that your values may change according to changes in your life. Be prepared also to modify your values according to different circumstances.

In a nutshell

- When your work matches your values, your work and career will feel compatible with who you are and what's important to you. You'll feel you're doing work that has meaning and purpose for you.
- Your core values are intrinsic values; they are the values you bring to a job, your work, your career. You will also have work values; these are extrinsic values. Extrinsic values are concerned with what you get out of your work, rather than what you put into it.
- Using your values to help you make decisions about work and a career to pursue means you're less likely to be influenced by what others think you 'ought' to do or 'should' do.
- Occasionally, you'll need to review your values. Your life and circumstances will go through changes and so what's important to you now might not be the same in the future.

3
Knowing Your Skills, Strengths, and Learning Styles

There are two ways of exerting one's strength: one is pushing down, the other is pulling up.

Booker T. Washington

According to research into human behavior published in 2014 by the analytics and advisory organization Gallup, when people know and use their strengths – their personal qualities and attributes – and when their employer encourages them to use their strengths, people are more engaged, perform better, have a stronger work ethic, more enthusiasm and commitment than those who have fewer opportunities to use their strengths at work. Gallup's research also shows that when a person is using their strengths at work, it leads to improved health and well-being outcomes; the more times each day a person can use their strengths to do what they do best, the less likely they are to report experiencing worry, stress, anger, or physical pain during the previous day.

It makes sense, then, to be working in a job or career that not only reflects your values, but also uses your strengths.

Identifying Your Qualities and Strengths

Read through this list and as you do, tick each and every quality that applies to you:

Adaptable and flexible: I'm able to change my approach and adjust to different conditions and circumstances.

Calm: I can deal with problems as they happen; I don't get over-excited or too anxious, angry, or upset when things go wrong.

Conscientious: I'm guided by a sense of what's right; I like to work carefully and do things thoroughly.

Cooperative: I work well with other people; I'm willing to be of assistance in working towards a common goal.

Decisive: I make decisions easily, with little hesitation.

Determined: I resolve to stick to a decision and/or keep going.

Enthusiastic: I have a keen interest in ideas, activities, tasks etc. I'm usually eager to get on with things.

Friendly: I'm open and welcoming to others.

Good-natured: I'm calm, patient, accepting, and easy-going.

Imaginative, creative, and innovative: I can come up with new ways and ideas to make things happen and get things done and to solve problems and overcome difficulties.

Logical: I'm capable of reasoning in a clear and consistent manner: I can easily work out what the next steps are.

Loyal: I can be trusted to stick with a person or cause, to be supportive.

Intuitive and perceptive: I'm insightful; I know when something does or doesn't feel right. I can read between the lines, pick up on what others are feeling – what their needs, likes, and dislikes are.

Methodical and organized: I have clear methods and systems for doing things in an orderly way. I plan things efficiently.

Observant: I'm quick to notice things. I notice details and I'm perceptive.

Open-minded: I'm willing to consider new ideas and different ways of doing things.

Optimistic: I'm usually hopeful and confident that things will turn out well.

Organized: I'm able to pull seemingly unrelated things together and create a sense of order. I plan and prioritize and I create methods and routines.

Patient: I can wait for things to happen in their own time. I can accept delay and difficulties without becoming annoyed or anxious.

Persistent: I can continue a course of action in spite of difficulty or opposition.

Practical and realistic: I like to do whatever works; whatever is effective and brings results. I'm more concerned with the actual doing or use of something rather than with theory and ideas. I'm sensible and realistic in my approach to a situation or problem.

Reliable: I can be trusted and depended on to keep my word, to do what I say I will, and to do something well.

Resourceful: I'm able to find quick and clever ways to deal with new situations and overcome difficulties.

Responsible and accountable: I can be trusted to do what I've said I'll do. Not only will I ensure the job is done, but I also accept responsibility for the results – good or bad. I don't make excuses or lay blame if something doesn't work out. I can explain, justify, and take responsibility.

Resilient: I can recover quickly from adversity, from difficulties and setbacks.

Thorough: I take pains to do something carefully and completely.

Trustworthy: I can be depended on to do something; I'm reliable.

* * * * *

Now, choose five of the qualities you've ticked: your top five strengths. For each of those five qualities, think some more about how each strength is, or could be, beneficial to you in a job.

For example, if you felt that patience was one of your qualities, you might recognize that at work, you don't rush things or overlook details; you take time to do things properly so that you don't make mistakes and you don't waste time having to go back over things.

If being imaginative and innovative are two of your strengths, you'll know that you can come up with new ways and ideas to make things happen and get things done. Can you think of times in the past when you've done that?

And if you're cooperative, you work well with other people. Write down a couple of examples of when you've been involved in activities, jobs, projects etc. where you have worked supportively with other people on something.

Identifying Your Work Skills

As well as personal strengths and qualities, we all have skills: abilities that come as a result of knowledge and/or experience and that we can do well. We also have skills that are talents: a natural ability to do something well, without any training or practice.

Maybe you have good written and verbal communication skills: you can clearly explain and understand ideas, opinions, thoughts, and feelings and you can succinctly tell others what does and doesn't need doing. Perhaps you have social and interpersonal skills: you can work cooperatively and collaboratively; you listen to others, share ideas, you can be tactful and persuasive; you're skilled at negotiating, motivating, supporting, and encouraging others. Perhaps you have research skills: you're good at finding relevant facts and information. Maybe you have good IT skills. Do you have any specific practical skills? Perhaps you're skilled at using particular equipment and tools.

Read through this list of work skills. Give each skill a score out of 10 according to how skilled you are in each of the following areas:

Creative, artistic skills: I can turn new and imaginative ideas into reality. I can interpret things in new, original ways – painting, poetry, sculpture, fashion, music, food, etc.

Numerical skills: I'm good with numbers; I can make calculations easily and accurately; I can easily understand and use the numerical techniques of mathematics.

Verbal communication skills: I can clearly explain ideas, opinions, thoughts, and feelings in a way that makes it easy for others to understand. I can clearly and succinctly tell others how to do something.

Practical skills: I can make, fix, and mend things using my hands and/or equipment and tools.

Organizing skills: I can pull disparate things together and create a sense of order. I plan and prioritize and I create methods and routines. I'm good at organizing people, arranging meetings and events.

Social and interpersonal skills: I'm cooperative and collaborative, I listen to others, share ideas, and can be tactful and persuasive. I'm good at negotiating, motivating, supporting, and encouraging others. I relate well to others on a one-to-one basis and/or I interact well with others in a group.

Problem-solving skills: I take a calm, logical approach to challenges and difficulties. I use reasoning and rationalizing as well as my imagination to find solutions to problems.

Physical skills: I have good physical coordination. I have good fine motor and/or gross motor skills. I have high levels of stamina, strength, and speed, and/or flexibility, agility, and balance.

Write down what specific skills you have. They could be work-related skills. But they don't have to be work-related skills. They could be skills you have developed as part of a special interest or hobby. And they don't have to be skills that you excel at. For any skill you have, you just need to be able to do it reasonably easily and well.

Ask family and friends what skills they think you have. What do they think you're good at?

What do you think your top three skills – or skill areas – are? For each skill, ask yourself, do I like doing this? The skills, abilities, and talents that you possess are not necessarily the ones you enjoy using. You may be really good at a particular sport or organizing other people to do things but, actually, you don't love doing it. What skills do you like and not like using? Again write them down.

Hidden Skills and Strengths

You probably know what you can do well, what you do and don't like doing, and you probably know what things that you don't do well at all; what skills and talents you don't have. But it's very likely that there are abilities you have that you haven't had the opportunity to discover. There are a number of things that you could be really good at if you had the opportunity to try and to practise.

You can think of your skills as being in three different categories; top 30%, bottom 20%, and middle 50%.

The bottom 20% can be dismissed as not worth putting in the time and effort to improve. Perhaps you are hopeless at mending and fixing things – you don't have the physical dexterity or the patience. You can put the skills you're no good at to one side.

The top 30% of your skills – the ones you enjoy using – are the ones you'd do well to utilize and develop further. However, the issue with only drawing on your top skills is that you can stay stuck in the same role, doing the same job or work. And it's likely that you'll be less open to learning new skills.

What about the middle 50% of skills and abilities? What are they all about? They are your hidden skills; they're simply things you haven't tried doing yet, but with focus, interest, and practice you could become quite good at them. They're skills that are just waiting to be developed.

In response to the ever-changing world of work, it's important not to rely only on what you can currently do well, but also develop new skills, strengths, and abilities. New circumstances and challenges will emerge, and staying on top means that you'll need to be open to developing new skills.

Even if there isn't an immediate need to learn new skills, be willing to try new experiences: trying new ways of doing things can uncover skills and abilities – the middle 50% – that you didn't even know you had. Once uncovered, developing those skills and abilities can open up new opportunities.

Identifying Your Learning Styles

Identifying your values, skills, strengths, and abilities can help you identify what job, work, or career would most likely match those attributes.

Did you know that, as well as having specific values, skills, strengths, and qualities, you have your own individual way of learning? The way that one person learns may be quite different from the way the next person learns.

To learn means to acquire new skills and knowledge. And we each have different ways of doing that. Imagine, for example, that you had to learn how to make, install, or mend something. Would you want to read the instructions first, think through each step, and then do it? Or would you just want to get stuck in and try different ways of doing something until you find the most successful? Some of us learn best by doing things first and then thinking about what happened, how to make sense of it, and what we've learnt from doing it. Others learn best by thinking things through first and then getting on with the doing.

In 1986, occupational psychologist Peter Honey and his colleague Alan Mumford – a management development advisor – identified four different learning styles: Activist, Pragmatist, Reflector and Theorist. These learning styles apply not just to how we learn, but also to our preferred way of doing things, of working.

If you're an activist you're someone who likes to get started on things straight away. You're happy to hit the ground running. You love the challenge of new experiences and you'll try anything once. You're open-minded and enthusiastic about learning and doing new things. You learn best – and are therefore happiest – when you can just get on with it, without any constraints. However, you have a tendency to do too much yourself. You may take unnecessary risks and rush into action without sufficient preparation. If things don't work out, instead of stopping to consider why, you often just move on to the next thing. You're impatient; you often don't consolidate – pull everything together at the end – and you leave things unfinished.

If your style of learning and doing things is that of a pragmatist, once you've understood an idea or theory, you're keen to try it out and put it into practice. You learn best when you can make practical decisions and, like activists, solve problems by getting straight on with things. However, you may tend to seize on the first convenient solution to a problem and although it might be practical, it's not always the best, most suitable or appropriate way to get things done.

If your preferred way of learning and doing is that of a theorist you take a logical, structured approach to everything you learn and do. You like to analyze and understand the theory behind ideas, concepts, and systems. You're organized and disciplined and likely to be a perfectionist. However, you don't like uncertainty, disorder, and ambiguity. You're not happy until things fit into a rational scheme; a systematic and logical theory. Your perfectionism can result in procrastination: you hold back from doing something for fear of not being able to do it perfectly.

If your style of learning and doing things is that of a reflector, you like to stand back and see things from different perspectives before doing anything. You're happy to observe and listen to others. You like harmony. You're ordered, careful, cautious, calm, methodical, and thorough. You learn best – and so therefore are more productive – if you can think first; do some research, gather views, opinions, ideas, and information. You like to do things in your own time without pressure and deadlines. You struggle when there's no time for planning and you don't have enough information to make a decision. You may have a tendency to procrastinate and you find it difficult to take short cuts.

You can find out for yourself what your preferred learning style is by Googling *Honey and Mumford Learning Style Questionnaire*. You will probably find that you're not 100% any one particular learning style; that you prefer different methods of learning and doing things, depending upon the situation.

Not only can each of these learning styles be seen to apply to how a person learns, but they also apply to how a person approaches the work they do: activities, tasks and projects.

It isn't that each of us can only learn or approach tasks and activities in one way, it's just that we might find one way easier than others. There are strengths and weaknesses to each style. The trick is to identify and make use of your strengths and to be aware of and work on, or around, your weaknesses. So, for example, you might be an activist – you're enthusiastic about learning and doing new things. You like to get started on things straight away and hit the ground running. In a team, working with others, that's a strength – to be the one that gets things going. But, you often don't consolidate – pull everything together at the end – and you leave things unfinished. A possible solution there is to have someone in the team who is happy to take your ideas and see them through to the end: a 'theorist' – someone who's more of a perfectionist and will tie up the loose ends.

Auditory, Kinaesthetic, Visual Learning

As well as the extent to which we learn and do best either by doing first or thinking first, we each have a preferred sensory way of learning and doing. This involves the extent to which you learn best by listening, seeing, or touch.

Tick the statements that best apply to you:

1. **What kinds of book do you like to read?**
   a. books that have a lot of descriptions
   b. books with a lot of dialogue in them
   c. books with plenty of action, not many descriptions
2. **When you have to spell a word you are not sure about you:**
   a. visualize the word in your head
   b. sound it out, in your head or out loud
   c. write the word to see if it feels right
3. **When you have the time do you prefer to:**
   a. watch TV, go to the cinema, or read
   b. listen to music, the radio, or podcasts
   c. take part in a sport, fix something, or make something
4. **After you've met someone for the first time are you more likely to:**
   a. forget their name but remember their face
   b. forget their face but remember their name
   c. forget names and faces, but remember what you did or what happened when you were with them

5. **Which of these do you enjoy most?**
   a. art exhibitions, paintings, or photographs
   b. listening to music
   c. dancing, going for a walk, or sport
6. **If you have a meeting do you:**
   a. go prepared with notes
   b. enjoy having a discussion and hearing what other people have to say
   c. spend your time fiddling with something or doodling
7. **When you try to imagine something, you:**
   a. see details very clearly and have a clear picture?
   b. hear sounds or what people are saying?
   c. do not see or hear much, but feel what is happening?
8. **When you are trying to concentrate you are likely to be:**
   a. distracted by untidiness
   b. distracted by sound or noise
   c. distracted by movement
9. **When you are learning, you:**
   a. like to read, see diagrams, demonstrations, or slides
   b. like having things explained to you, like lectures or talks
   c. like role play, making things, games or puzzles
10. **When you're at a live music event, you:**
    a. watch the band members and people in the audience

     b. listen to the lyrics and the beat

     c. dance and move around to the music

11. **When you put together a new piece of furniture or equipment do you:**

     a. read the instructions thoroughly before you begin and as you go along

     b. watch someone do it on YouTube

     c. just go ahead and figure it out as you go; trial and error

Add all the ticks together for each letter and see which letter you have the most ticks for. This will show you what kind of learner you are.

Mostly a: you are a visual learner

Mostly b: you are an auditory learner

Mostly c: you are a kinaesthetic learner

Visual learners actually think in images or pictures. They visualize what they hear or read; it's as if though they have a camera in their mind. When you want to recall what you've learnt, you look upwards and look at the images you have on a 'screen'. This is much like describing a film to someone else.

You prefer to write down directions and you pay better attention to lectures if you watch them. Visual learners do well with charts, demonstrations, videos, and other visual materials.

You probably like to use colour highlighters and take notes by drawing pictures, diagrams, or doodling. You easily visualize faces and places by using your imagination and seldom get lost in new surroundings.

Auditory learners learn best by listening. You like discussions and prefer talking to writing and reading. Auditory learners often talk to themselves and read out loud to 'hear' information as they commit it to memory.

Written information has little meaning until it's been 'heard' or listened to; as an auditory learner, you may need to repeat instructions out loud or to yourself. Easily distracted by noises, you may work better with background music to muffle other unwanted sounds or lack of sound. You can get bored or restless if work or study has to be done in silence. With meetings and talks you tend to listen first then take notes afterwards.

Kinaesthetic learners do best while touching and moving. If they can physically interact with what they are learning then they will retain the new knowledge or information well.

You tend to lose concentration if there is little or no external stimulation or movement. When listening to lectures you may want to take notes for the sake of moving your hands. When writing, it's likely that you press hard on the paper to 'feel' the words. When reading, you like to scan the material first, and then focus in on the details (get the big picture first). You might use colour highlighters and take notes by drawing pictures, diagrams, or doodling.

Kinaesthetic learners often talk about their learning in terms of their feelings and how something makes them feel.

You get restless if you have to sit still for too long; you need to stand up or have space to move around. You find it difficult to focus and concentrate; you find formal classroom environments a challenge. You can be impulsive. When you come across new equipment and gadgets, you are keen to try them out.

Once you've identified your values, strengths, skills, and learning styles, write them all down on the same page. Here's an example of how that could look:

Strengths
Loyal – I can be trusted to stick with a person or cause; to be supportive

Friendly – I'm open and welcoming to others

Good-natured – I'm calm, patient, accepting, and easy-going

Trustworthy – I can be depended on to do something; I'm reliable

Organized – I'm able to pull seemingly unrelated things together and create a sense of order. I plan and prioritize and I create methods and routines

Values
Family, Dependability, Kindness, Love, Optimism

Work values
Social: working with others. Environment: pleasant physical surroundings. Economic: well-paid

Work skills
Influencing, Verbal Communication, Organizing, Practical

Learning styles
Activist. Kinaesthetic

Can you see what this person's key traits are?

The key traits of this person are that they are sociable and organized.

Having written down your values, skills etc., you'll have a picture that illustrates who you are; what's important to you in the way you live in the world and interact with others, and what's important for you to get from the work you do. You'll also have identified your attributes – your strengths – and your skills – what you're good at doing. And you'll have pinpointed the way that you naturally approach learning and doing.

In a nutshell

- When you're able to use your strengths – your personal qualities and attributes – you're more likely to work well, to be interested and engaged with your work, to enjoy and be satisfied at work.

- As well as personal strengths and qualities, you have skills and talents. Be aware of what skills and talents you have; which ones you do and don't like using.
- Being open to learning new things; trying new experiences and new ways of doing things can uncover skills and abilities that you didn't even know you had. Once uncovered, developing those skills and abilities can open up new opportunities for you.
- You have your own individual way of learning and doing. The way you learn – the way you acquire new skills and knowledge – may be different from the way the next person learns and does things.
- Identifying your values, skills, strengths, and abilities can help you identify what job, work, or career would most likely match those attributes.

4
Identifying Possible Jobs and Careers

I could be the driver of an articulated lorry
I could be a poet
I wouldn't need to worry
I could be a teacher in a classroom full of scholars
I could be the sergeant in a squadron full of wallahs
I could be a lawyer with stratagems and ruses
I could be a doctor with poultices and bruises
I could be a writer with a growing reputation
I could be the ticket man at Fulham Broadway Station.
                    Ian Dury and Roderick Martin Melvin

Turning an Interest into a Career

What do you like doing? What are you interested in? Is there something that you really enjoy doing; that keeps you interested and engaged, that you spend quite a lot of time doing and learning more about? Did you have a favourite subject at school – whether you left school last year or many years ago – was there one or more subjects you particularly enjoyed?

Do you have any hobbies? Perhaps you enjoy fishing or birdwatching? Perhaps you like watching or playing football? It could be gardening that you enjoy. Going to festivals or throwing parties. Maybe it's hiking or skiing or running marathons. Perhaps you enjoy playing computer games, reading novels, watching films, or singing in a choir. Maybe you're fascinated by pond life or Victorian oil paintings.

Have you thought about doing what you enjoy doing – what interests or fascinates you – as a job or career?

Pretty much any interest can be turned into paid work and a career. If you enjoy model-making, for example, you could be a prop maker creating objects for use in theatre, film, and TV productions. If you really enjoy reading, you could be a book editor commissioning authors to write books, or a proofreader or subeditor, checking and editing written documents, articles and books. Of course there's more to being a subeditor or proofreader than a love of reading. And there's more to being a prop maker than enjoying model making. But the main thing is knowing that having an interest in something *could* (but doesn't have to) lead to a career in that area.

Perhaps you love graphic novels but think you couldn't make a living out of graphic novels. Actually, you could: you could be a comic book or graphic novel illustrator, you could publish comic books and graphic novels, you could work in marketing for a comic book or graphic novel publisher. You could work in a shop that sells comic books and graphic novels. Someone does. Why not you? It could be that you're into trainspotting. Is there a job doing that? Maybe not. But there are plenty of opportunities to work on the railways. Or with a railway preservation line. Are you are a keen birdwatcher? The Royal Society for the Protection of Birds (RSPB) has around 1,500 paid staff; there could be a job – a career – there for you.

There are lots of ways you can combine skills and interests. Perhaps you feel strongly about climate change. And you enjoy writing; you're good at it. So you could be a journalist writing about climate change and green issues.

Perhaps you're interested in children's learning – in how children learn – but you don't want to be a schoolteacher. Are there any other paths open to you? Yes, there are. You could, for example, have a career as an educational psychologist.

Maybe you've thought about turning an interest or hobby into a job or a career but haven't done anything about it because you've dismissed the idea as unviable; you think it wouldn't pay enough or you'd have to study and get qualifications, or friends and family might think your idea is ridiculous. Or you don't know how to get into it; where to start and what further steps to take. Whatever the reason, you just don't think it's a realistic option. Most likely, though, your assumptions about why you couldn't turn a passion, interest, or hobby into a job or career are just that – assumptions: beliefs that have little in the way of evidence to support them. Before you dismiss a particular line of work or career as unviable, you need to find out more about ways into it or how you *could* make it work for you.

In the next chapter we'll look at how you can start turning a passion or interest into a job or career. But for now, if you do have one or more interests or a passion for something, just write them down and then, in Chapters 5 and 6 you'll read how turning a passion or interest into a career can become a reality.

Should You Make Your Passion Your Work?

Of course, just because you have an interest or a passion for something, it doesn't mean you have to turn it into how you earn your living. You might want to keep it as something you do that's separate from work; for some people, turning an interest or hobby into work changes it from a 'love to do' to a 'have to do'. Or you *have* done your research and actually, for you, turning an interest or hobby you have into a job or career really *isn't* viable.

A different way to satisfy values

Carla worked for an accountancy company. She was highly paid and enjoyed her work; it provided all the things that were important to her in a job – authority and responsibility, reliability, accountability, control – but over the last year, Carla felt that something was missing.

Although her core values and work values hadn't changed – her job continued to be enjoyable and engage her – Carla had a set of values – social values – that weren't being fulfilled by her work. Carla wanted to be doing something that would enable her to make a positive difference to other people's lives; she wanted to be involved in contributing directly to other people's lives in a fun, active way. She researched other professions and careers but discovered that if she wanted to work in a hands-on role there was little, if anything, that would provide the same high-level salary she was paid in her current job.

Carla remembered how much she'd enjoyed being in the Girl Guides when she was a teenager so she contacted Girlguiding to find out what opportunities there might be for her to get involved as an adult. She was invited to train to be a Unit Leader, responsible for setting up and running a local Girl Guides group, leading a team, planning and taking part in a programme of fun activities and events. Within a few months, amongst other activities, Carla had organized and led a kayaking weekend for a group of Girl Guides. And Carla stayed in her job: a win-win situation!

What if There Isn't Anything You Feel Inspired to Do?

It could be that you don't have a particular passion or interest to pursue as a job or career; there isn't anything you feel particularly inspired to do. Is there something wrong with you? Of course not! You're not the problem; the problem is the belief that there *is* a dream job or career out there for each of us, that we were each born to do and devote ourselves to doing for all our working lives.

Perhaps you're hoping that once you've found your 'calling' everything else will fall into place. Certainly, some people do appear to have a 'calling'; they're compelled to pursue a particular career which they dedicate themselves to and enjoy doing throughout their life.

But who says you have to have a job that you love, that's your calling, your passion? It's unrealistic to think that you'll have job or career which starts with you waking up every single day dancing out of your pyjamas to do it. Yes, there may be a dream job out there waiting for you, but you can spend a lot of time and energy looking for it and if you are unable to find it, you risk feeling continually disappointed.

Your ideal job or career isn't necessarily something you find, it's something you create. Other people's 'successful' careers often have paths that belie the idea that all you have to do is follow your passion.

Many people who really enjoy their work do so and have got there as a result of trying something, discovering they like it, and developing their interest, skills, knowledge, and experience from there. They've put their time and energy into making their work or career work for them. You can do the same.

You don't *have* to have a calling, a big idea, or a long-term career plan. Instead, you need to identify what *might* be of interest and be a good direction, take one step at a time, and learn from what you find out along the way.

Identify the Jobs and Careers that Might Be of Interest to You

So, the next step is to identify jobs and careers that could be of interest and appeal to you. Write down any job, profession, or career you can think of that appeals to you. If it's a little bit interesting, write it down. If you have a dream job, write it down. At this stage, don't worry about how much it might pay, what other people might think about you doing it, what qualifications you might need – if you think it could be right for you, write it down.

Then, look through this random list of jobs. Without thinking too much about each one – the hours, the pay, or the social status – tick any job that appeals to you:

Firefighter
Architect
Chef
Barber
Doctor
Art historian
Bricklayer
Gardener

Veterinary nurse
Accountant
Café owner
Wedding and events
    photographer
Paramedic
Farmer
Sports coach

Train driver	Car mechanic
Counsellor	Jet pilot
Journalist	Social worker
Tech engineer	Conservationist of art
Research scientist	and furniture
Musician	Novelist
Care home manager	Estate agent
Interior designer	Locksmith
Events organizer	

Now, briefly write down what you think you'd like about each job you've ticked. Do you think it would be interesting? Exciting? There'd be good promotion prospects? For each job you've ticked, in what ways does it match your values, your skills and strengths? Write it all down. Think about what you chose and why? Do the jobs and careers you've ticked have a common thread? Do they, for example, involve working on your own? Are a number of the roles that interest you creative roles? Or working with vulnerable people?

It might not be immediately obvious how your skills and strengths match up with a job or particular profession. You may need to think through how you could bring your particular strengths and abilities to that work. Having a good sense of humour, for example – that doesn't mean you have to be a comedian, but for any job working with other people, a sense of humour is always going to be needed! And an interest in the arts and drama could, for example, be an asset if you were interested in being a care home manager: you'd be able to run a programme of activities and entertainment for the care home residents.

As well as asking yourself, 'What work might I like, find interesting, and enjoy doing?' it's helpful to think about what jobs – what work – you would *not* enjoy doing. Briefly write down what you think you'd dislike about each job that you didn't tick in the list on pages 67 & 68. Do you think it would be boring? Scary? Did you not tick some of those jobs because it would mean working irregular hours and that wouldn't suit you? For each job you haven't ticked, in what ways does it *not* reflect your values, your skills and strengths? Write it all down.

Next, have a look at the job profiles on the following websites. You can read firsthand accounts from people who are doing the jobs that interest you. The jobs profile pages on these websites are a really good resource for getting more information about specific job roles and responsibilities, the skills and qualifications required, and the rate of pay. You'll also discover jobs and careers that you didn't even know existed!

- UCAS https://www.ucas.com/ucas/after-gcses/find-career-ideas/explore-jobs
- Prospects https://www.prospects.ac.uk/job-profiles/browse-a-to-z
- BBC Careers https://www.bbc.co.uk/bitesize/articles/zdqnxyc/

Add to your list of jobs that appeal to you any that you like the sound of from reading about them on these websites.

Write down any further ideas on what you think you'd like about each job you've ticked. Do you think it would be interesting? Exciting? There'd be good promotion prospects? For each job you've ticked, in what ways does it match your values, your skills and strengths? Write it all down.

Now that you've identified some possible jobs and careers, as well as the criteria to judge them by – the extent to which they match your interests, values, skills, and strengths – the next step, explained in Chapter 5, is to find out about them in more detail. If you've got a long list of potential jobs and careers, don't worry if there seem to be too many or they're too disparate. The next step – finding out more information about those roles – will help you to narrow down your list.

In a nutshell

- Before you dismiss a particular line of work or career as unviable, you need to find out more about ways into it or how you *could* make it work for you.
- Just because you have an interest or a passion for something, it doesn't mean you have to turn it into your job or career. You might want to

keep it as something you do that's separate from work.

- It could be that you *don't* have a particular passion or interest that you'd like to pursue as a job or career; there isn't anything you feel particularly inspired to do.

- You don't *have* to have a calling, a big idea, or a long-term career plan. Your ideal job or career is something you create; you identify what might be of interest and be a good direction, take one step at a time, and learn from what you find out along the way.

- Many people who really enjoy their work do so and have got there as a result of trying something; discovering they like it and developing their interest, skills, knowledge, and experience from there. They've put their time and energy into making their work or career work for them. You can do the same.

- For any job or career that appeals to you, at this stage, don't worry about how much it might pay, what other people might think about you doing it, what qualifications you might need. If you think it could be right for you, write it down.

- Think about what you'd like about each job. In what ways does it match your values, skills, and strengths?

- As well as asking yourself, 'What work might I like, find interesting, and enjoy doing?' it's helpful to think about what jobs – what work – you would *not* enjoy doing. In what ways does it *not* reflect your values, your skills and strengths? Write it all down.

- Once you've identified some possible jobs and careers, as well as the criteria to judge them by – the extent to which they match your interests, values, skills, and strengths – the next step is to find out about them in more detail.

5
Finding Out More About the Work that Interests You

Don't be afraid to ask questions. Don't be afraid to ask for help when you need it. I do that every day. Asking for help isn't a sign of weakness, it's a sign of strength. It shows you have the courage to admit when you don't know something, and to learn something new.

Barack Obama

Once you've identified one or more jobs or careers that might be of interest you, the next step is to find out more about each specific job or role so that you can clarify or revise your ideas, possibilities, and options. There are a number of ways you can do this; you can set up some 'informational interviews' with people who are doing the work that you're interested in, you could organize to work shadow one or more people as they do their job, or find a voluntary role in the area that interests you.

Informational Interviews

Whatever you're interested in – working as a dog trainer or a train driver, an Uber driver or Deliveroo delivery person, training to be a midwife or a geriatric nurse, an astronomer or a tarot card reader – a good way to find out more about a job or profession – whether it's as an employee, working freelance, or starting your own business – is to talk to someone who is already doing it or has recently done it. If it's a particular company you're interested in working for, talking to someone who works there or has recently worked there can also provide useful insights and information.

You'll need to do some 'informational interviews'. An informational interview simply involves talking to someone – asking them questions – about their work or career. You may already know quite a bit about a certain role or job, but speaking to people who are or have recently been doing the work you're interested in can help you find out a lot more about the type of industry, company, job, or career.

Yes, it can be a difficult step reaching out to people you don't know; certainly, some people might be reluctant to chat to you – but you'll be surprised at how often some people *are* willing to give you half an hour or more of their time, either by phone, email, or in person, to talk about their job or their business and give their advice.

Who to Meet and Where to Find Them

Where to find people you could talk to who are doing the work you're interested in? Start with your own, informal network. The people in your own informal network could be:

- Friends, family, or neighbours
- Colleagues and ex-colleagues
- Fellow students on the same course as you or people who you went to school, college, or university with
- Members of clubs or teams you're in
- People who you know through voluntary work you do
- Members of the same church, mosque, synagogue, or religious community you belong to
- An online community you belong to.

Ask people in your informal network if anyone they know does the work you're interested in and would be willing to put you in touch with them. And if you're still in education, find out whether your school or college has a list of possible contacts for people you could talk to now, and later, for work shadowing opportunities.

Find out who knows who

Julia is in the same book club as Alana. It came up in conversation that Julia's sister is an expert horsewoman. A few weeks later, Alana's nephew

---

mentioned that he'd always wanted to learn to ride a horse. Alana phoned Julia and asked if her sister would be able to give a private lesson, because she wanted to give it to him as a birthday gift. Julia's sister agreed and Alana's nephew was thrilled. A while later, Julia needed some help marketing her new business. Alana's nephew's girlfriend is a freelance social media marketing consultant; Julia employs her. Alana's nephew's girlfriend is very grateful and, in return, introduces Alana to a photographer who takes some excellent photos for the website Alana is designing for her new business.

Outside of your informal network, there are a number of ways you can find people and make contact with them. Google is a good start. If it's a specific job – children's entertainer, or dog walker, or plumber, or electrician, for example – simply Google children's entertainer, dog walker, plumber, or electrician.

If you want to start your own business or work freelance, begin by looking for people who are running a similar business. In some cases, you'll have to talk to people in a different area from where you live. If, for example, you were thinking of opening a barbers or hairdressers, or setting up as a bike repair service, talking to someone in the same town or village as yours wouldn't be a good idea; they'd see you as competition and a threat to their business! But if you wanted to work freelance as an illustrator, it wouldn't matter if one of the illustrators you talked to lived in the same street, as you'll most likely have different specialisms – your neighbour's illustrations could be for corporate work – brochures, catalogues, websites. Your interest might be in merchandising – greeting cards, calendars, t-shirts, ceramics.

Whether you're aiming to set up your own business or you're interested in a particular paid role, profession, or career, with only a person's name, you can Google them, look at their LinkedIn profile, their Facebook page, their Instagram account, and, if they Tweet, their Twitter stream.

LinkedIn – a networking website for people in professional jobs – is a valuable resource. LinkedIn lets you create an online profile like a CV to highlight your skills and the things you've done. It also allows you to:

- connect with other individuals and groups
- research companies
- look for jobs.

Use LinkedIn to find and contact people doing the work you're interested in. Look out for any connection you might have with someone; if they went to the same college or university, or you share some other connection, they may be more open to meeting with you.

If there's a particular company you're interested in working for or a particular role with a company, go to their website and see if they have a page titled 'Our people' or 'About us' or 'Contact us'. Find the relevant person and contact them.

Another way to find and make contact with people working in a particular job or career is to find out is to discover whether the area you're interested in has a professional association. If, for example, you're interested in forestry and woodland management, The Institute of Chartered Foresters has a website: www.charteredforesters.org. The website has a 'Hire a Consultant' page from which you could locate a forestry business in your area; you could get in touch to ask if you could meet up with someone from the business to find out more about their work.

Networking events are a good place to meet people in the profession or career that appeals to you. Going to a business social or an association meeting or event and approaching people you don't already know might seem daunting at first. What to say? What to ask? What if they say no? If you need practice chatting to strangers, try https://dialup.com/. Whether it's discussing what book you're reading, what you're making for breakfast, the full moon, or world affairs, Dialup will ring your phone and another Dialup member's phone on an automated schedule and pair you randomly in a one-on-one conversation.

Do keep in mind, though, that networking events aren't about walking into a room full of strangers and trying to charm them all. They're business events specifically organized for people to meet each other. So people *will* be open to you introducing yourself.

Most industries hold regular networking events. These usually have a programme of relevant talks interspersed with time to meet and talk with others at the event. They're designed to help businesses and individuals to increase their professional networks so that they can create opportunities and partnerships.

Training courses and conferences can also be a good way to meet people from other organizations; you can get to know them during the breaks.

Look for events for the professions you're interested in. For example, the Royal Society https://royalsociety.org/ is the UK's national academy of sciences, dedicated to promoting excellence in science. Their Summer of Science event offers a programme of talks. And – another example – the Women's Engineering Society www.wes .org.uk/ is a professional network of women engineers, scientists, and technologists offering inspiration, support, and professional development. They organize conferences and webinars.

You can often find out about local events from the Chamber of Commerce – The Chamber of Commerce Network www.britishchambers.org.uk/ supports and connects people and companies, bringing them together to build new relationships, share best practice, and foster new opportunities. They all run training and networking events.

Jobs and careers fairs are also good places to meet and talk to people. They are either specific to a profession or industry – for example, nursing have the RCN Nursing Careers and Jobs Fair www.careersandjobsfair.com/ – or they involve a variety of different employers from various industries. Careers and jobs fairs are often free to attend. You can register with employers for jobs, collect information on employers, ask them questions, apply for jobs, and even have a short interview on the day. Have a look at www.thejobfairs.co.uk/.

Find someone doing the same thing you want to do

Jo was interested in setting up a community magazine that would cover local news, history, local people, and upcoming events in her small town and surrounding area. She thought that the magazine could make money – and therefore provide an income for Jo – by selling advertising space in the magazine. Although there was already a community magazine for the area of the large town Jo lived in, she thought it was badly designed and that most of the articles were uninteresting. While visiting a friend in a small town 50 miles from where she lived, Jo picked up a copy of a community magazine that was exactly like the one she envisaged for her area. She arranged to meet with Steve, who ran the magazine, and pick his brains; Steve gave Jo a wealth of advice, information, and contacts. Jo was further encouraged when, in answer to her concern that there was already a community magazine in her area, Steve told her 'It doesn't matter!

Whenever you're doing something that someone else is already doing, you just make what you're offering, much much better!'

Make Contact

Making contact and asking to meet up with someone you've not met before might feel a little bit scary. But the worst that can happen is that they won't respond or will respond with a 'No'. You can help make it more likely they'll agree to talk with you if you do two things: be clear and succinct about why you're getting in touch and about what you're asking from the other person. Don't make them guess how best to help you; you need to make it easy for them to agree to talk with you. Say what you're interested in and why – briefly let the person know what you already know and have found out – this will show you are genuine and sincere about wanting to know more.

Be specific: not just 'I'm interested in being a photographer'. What type of photographer would you like to be? A portrait photographer? A wedding photographer? A medical photographer?

People are more likely to meet and talk with you if they know you've done some research and you've got some knowledge – even just a little – about the role, profession, industry, and so on. The job profiles from the Prospects, UCAS, and BBC's Careers website pages mentioned on page 69 can help you here.

Offer to meet in person or online, on the phone, or just by email.

Example email

Hello ...

How you found them: I found your contact details on the *Film Crews R Us* website/your LinkedIn page/your website/your company's website/a professional association/directory/my cousin.

Some information about yourself: I'm in my final year at Ravensbourne University studying for a degree in Theatre and Performance Practice BA (Hons).

What exactly you're interested in: I'm aspiring to work as an assistant director in film and TV.

What you've already found out: I understand that to get into the film and TV industry I'd need to start as a runner or production assistant and I know it's not easy to get an 'in'. I also understand that the work involves long hours – early starts and late finishes – but I'm very keen and would like to know more. I'd really like to find out more about your role as a runner: what the work involves, what's a typical day and week, and any advice you could give me about how to get work as a runner.

What you're asking for; how and when to meet: I imagine you're busy so any time you could spare would be really appreciated. Either to meet up for a

---

coffee in the day or a drink in the evening. Or to talk over the phone or online. Or, perhaps I could email you a few questions?

Hope to hear back from you,

Regards, Gill Hasson

If you don't hear back right away, that's OK; people are busy. Don't just give up though; often people forget and may need a nudge. If they don't reply, follow up a week or ten days later; forward your first email and say:

Hello … I'm not sure if you received my email last week (below) so I'm just getting in touch again to see if you would be free to meet up/talk on the phone?

If I don't hear back, I'll assume you're not free.

Regards, Gill Hasson

If you still don't get a reply, don't take it personally or let it knock you back. Cast a wide net; find several people to contact so if one doesn't reply you've got other people to contact. Hopefully, you will contact more than one person anyway; the more different perspectives you have, the better informed you'll be.

If someone you've emailed replies with a no – then reply with 'Thanks for letting me know; is there anyone else you could recommend that I speak to?' It might feel a bit pushy on your part – but what's to lose? And your persistence shows that you're keen!

Prepare Some Questions

It's important to have clear, specific questions ready. That means doing some research and not wasting their time or yours with things you can easily find out elsewhere. Below are the types of question you could ask. You might ask all of them if you are talking with the other person. But if you're going to email, five questions is enough for them to have to type up their answers, so questions 2, 3, 4, 5, and 12 are probably the most useful to ask.

During your meeting do take notes. Simply say: 'I'm not going to remember everything you tell me so I'm going to take a few notes – hope that's ok?'

1. Have you always worked in this role/profession/ industry?

   If you know the other person's work history already and noticed any changes in career direction, you might also ask, for example, 'I saw from your LinkedIn page that you've worked at Company A and Company B. How did you go from Company A/position A to company B/position B?' The other person's answer can help you understand how their career path could lead to this role you're interested in.

2. How did you get into this line of work/profession/job?

3. What does a typical day or week at work look like for you?

4. What do you enjoy most about your job/work/career?
5. What do you like least or find the most difficult or challenging?

   It could be the mundane, everyday tasks, it might be office politics or the commute. Maybe it's a lack of support from management. Maybe it's physically or emotionally demanding. Whatever it is, think about whether this is something that you'd find difficult, too.

6. How, if at all, do you see this job changing in the next five years?

   The answer to this will give you an insight into the future and what you'll need to do to keep up and stay ahead of the game.

7. As far as your career/job is concerned, if you could go back and do anything differently, what would you do?

8. How do you continue learning – developing your skills and knowledge?

9. Do you belong to any professional organizations?

10. Do you have any advice about what the next steps might be for me?

    This assumes you've told the other person where you're currently at with regards to the work you're interested in.

11. Where do the vacancies in your profession get advertised?

12. Is there anyone else you'd suggest that I speak with about this line of work/company?

Do ask this last question! If the other person can recommend one or two more people and put you in touch with them, it's to your benefit. Although they might suggest someone else in the same role, different people doing the same jobs may have different answers to your questions as they'll have a different path, experience perspective, and opinions about their role. It could, though, be someone in an associated role that they recommend you talk with. For example, if you're interested in journalism, the journalist you talk to might suggest a subeditor or a section editor at the newspaper they work at.

The more people you can talk to, the more informed you'll be; the more directions and options you'll be aware of. Once you start connecting with people, you'll find that one thing leads to another. An added benefit of informational interviews is that you'll be building a network of contacts that may be useful in future. People who are willing to take the time to help you are people you need to keep as contacts. So if, having talked with them, you're still interested in the role or profession, do ask to connect with them on LinkedIn.

Be sure to thank the person for their time; the only thing in it for them is helping you. That's it. Send them a Thank You email or text; mention what you found most interesting/surprising or helpful to learn from them. If you do pursue the work or career they told you about, do send an update on your progress.

Having talked to someone – hopefully more than one person – about the job/work/career that you're interested in, you'll have a clearer idea of what it might involve: the potential pros and cons. The next step is to actually see for yourself.

Work Shadowing

Work shadowing is an opportunity to get more of an insight into a particular job or line of work or workplace; it involves spending time with a person at their job. Work shadowing brings a job to life and can help you decide whether it really is for you. If you can shadow more than one person it also allows you to see how the same job can be different depending on its setting. For example, the difference between working as a teacher in a primary school and working as a teacher in a secondary school. Or the difference between the work of a journalist who writes news reports compared to a journalist who writes film reviews.

The purpose of shadowing is to achieve an insight rather than to gain hands-on, practical experience.

Work shadowing is usually only for a day or two or two half-days. You could be watching what someone does on a typical day at work or you might shadow a person at work for a specific aspect of their job.

One thing leads to another

Ali had been working for a number of years in his role as marketing manager for a restaurant chain.

He wanted to do something different, but wasn't sure what else he really wanted to do.

Ali liked working with people but he also wanted to be involved in something that made a positive difference to other people's lives. One of his ideas was life coaching. So, his first step was to attend a coach training weekend. The training didn't cost anything (being offered free as a way to recruit people for paid-for courses) and it gave him the opportunity to find out more. Even before the end of the weekend, though, Ali knew it wasn't for him as it would have taken a lot of time and effort to build up a client base.

Something else Ali had considered was to continue working in marketing but for a charity – a third-sector organization. His friend Ellie's partner Meera worked as a charity fundraiser so Ali met her to find out more about her role. Meera explained how she got into charity fundraising, what her job involved day-to-day, the pros and cons of the work, and how it differed from the other different types of charity fundraising roles.

It all sounded good so Ali asked Meera – and she agreed – if he could shadow her in her role at work. Ali came away inspired after his day shadowing Meera. He looked at charitable organizations in his area and found that his local community hall was looking for someone, in a voluntary role, to help write bids for trust and grant money and to get involved in a variety of fundraising activities.

Taking on this role for the community hall helped Ali to build knowledge and experience and positioned him well, as and when the time was right for him, to make a bigger jump into a paid role in charity fundraising.

Some jobs are not suitable for shadowing due to the nature of the work and issues around health, confidentiality, and safety. It may not be possible to shadow someone who works in law or construction, for example. It also wouldn't be possible to shadow some healthcare roles – physical and mental healthcare roles or social care. If that's the case, an informational interview would be more appropriate. You could also get some hands-on experience by volunteering in a related role. For example, you wouldn't be able to work shadow a paramedic but you could get some experience training to be an Ambulance Service volunteer, a first responder, an event first aider, or a stadium first aider with St John Ambulance sja.org .uk/. Or as a volunteer for the Red Cross, an emergency response volunteer, or specialist NHS volunteer redcross.org.uk/.

To find the right person or people to work shadow, read the advice 'Who to meet and where to find them' on page 77.

Once you've identified someone and the role you'd like to know more about, you'll need to email the person or the organization explaining why you would like to shadow that person, or someone in that organization, doing the work you're interested in. Explain any processes you'd like to see or departments you'd like to view. This shows you've done your research and are genuinely keen. Explain, too, how you feel this could benefit you. It will need some organization by the person being shadowed, so a genuine interest from you in the role and their work is a must.

Example email

Hello ...

How you found them: I found your contact details on your LinkedIn page/your website/your company's website/a professional association/directory/my cousin.

Some information about yourself and what exactly you're interested in: I've always enjoyed gardening and am interested in changing careers, having spent the last 15 years working in retail, to train and work as a landscape gardener.

What you've already found out: I'm currently enrolled on the RHS Level 2 Diploma in the Principles and Practices of Horticulture which starts in September.

What you're asking for: I'm getting in touch to ask if I could spend a day with you in your job, work shadowing you, so that I can see what a typical day might

---

be like and also talk to you about your job. As you work for a specialist rose grower and I'm passionate about roses, I'd be very pleased to be able to spend some time with you in your work.

If you have a day in the next month that would be convenient for you, I could arrange to take holiday time from my job in order to spend the day work shadowing you.

Hope to hear back from you,

Regards, Gill Hasson

If you get a positive response and you do get to work shadow the person you contacted, during your time with them you just need to watch what they do and how they do it. Whether there's specific time for questions or you ask them throughout the day, it would be helpful to have some prepared. The person you're shadowing will still have to carry out their work while you're with them so be aware that they may not have a lot of time to answer. If there isn't any time for them to answer your queries, ask if it would be okay to email some follow-up questions.

Follow up by writing an email thanking them for the opportunity – for any particular effort they made to accommodate you and make you feel welcome. Explain what you found most helpful, interesting, or surprising. If the work, the role, or the company is still of interest and something you intend to pursue, keep in touch with the person you were shadowing; ask to connect with them on LinkedIn.

From head chef to community carer

In May 2020, 49-year-old David Lewis decided to leave his previous role managing a portfolio of high-end restaurants in Bristol, to become a community carer with Brunelcare, a charity providing care and support services for elderly people. He made the decision to swap the pots and pans for PPE at the start of the coronavirus pandemic.

David explains: 'My previous role was very stressful, very demanding and wasn't rewarding. After the hospitality business shut down at the start of the pandemic, I knew I had to re-evaluate my career path. I have been a chef for over 25 years and even though it was my passion, I knew I wanted to do something that really made a difference.'

David had previously volunteered at a homeless shelter and special schools across Bristol and had looked after friends and family members with learning difficulties. He spent two months shadowing senior community carers and undertaking training to become a qualified community carer with Brunelcare.

David says: 'When I saw the job advert for a community carer I knew it was right for me straight away. I don't have any official care training, but Brunelcare provided all that for me, all for free, it was great. I'm now conducting home visits with senior community carers and I absolutely love it! I feel I'm making a real difference!'

Volunteering

Volunteers can do almost anything! Whether it's bookkeeping for a community organization, stewarding at a music festival, working as a farm hand at a city farm, organizing a street party, rebuilding drystone walls, working with refugees, advocating for someone with a learning disability or mental health problem, or mentoring people leaving the criminal justice system – where there's a paid job, there's a similar or related voluntary role.

As well as making a worthwhile contribution to other people and/or the environment, voluntary work can help you to:

- Find out more about a specific industry or profession and give you an insight into an area of work you are interested in.
- Learn new skills; gain the skills needed to pursue a particular career – for example, working with children if you are interested in teaching.
- Acquire specific skills to further your career. You might, for example, want to move into a supervisory role as a team leader at work. Leading and

supervising others in a voluntary role will help give you the skills and experience you'd need.

- Build confidence and give you a sense of purpose.
- Gain practical experience, if you're studying, to complement those studies. For example, if you're studying to be a social worker and hope to work with substance misusers in future, volunteering with the relevant organization will give you hands-on experience.
- Meet new people, make connections, and build your network; show your interest and commitment to that area of work on your CV and to potential employers.
- Get a reference for future job applications.

Working as a volunteer for an organization could very well lead to a paid job within that organization. For many employers, it's not so important *where* you developed the skills, knowledge, or experience, it's the fact that you *do have* skills, knowledge, and experience and that you were proactive in getting them. It can help you to stand out from others. It shows you have initiative and are obviously keen on the role, profession, or industry.

Voluntary work can lead to a paid job

A number of years ago, when Georgia's children were very young, Georgia volunteered to be a 'home visitor' with the National Portage Association. Portage is a home-visiting educational service for pre-school

---

children with additional support needs and their families. Georgia received training and worked as a volunteer visitor for three years. Several years later, having trained to be an adult education tutor, Georgia applied for and was successful in getting a job teaching a qualification in childcare and child development to pre-school practitioners. Chatting with her manager Aamnah, some months later, Aamnah admitted that, amongst the other people they interviewed, what gave Georgia the edge and got her the job were the skills, knowledge, and experience she had acquired from volunteering as a Portage home visitor.

Most volunteer jobs come with training. And, more often than not, the training is free. Volunteer mediators with Brighton and Hove Independent Mediator Service (BHIMS), for example, are trained volunteers who, working in pairs, give their time to support people experiencing disputes in their community.

BHIMS says that volunteers don't need to have any special qualifications or experience to train as a mediator. They look for people who are good listeners and are able to support people without taking sides or making judgements. The service generally recruits and trains volunteer mediators every two years. The training is approved by the College of Mediators. It's a six-day course, usually run one or two days a week.

BHIMS supports all volunteers as they work on cases, with practical arrangements and case discussions.

They run monthly peer support sessions for mediators, providing the space to share the ups and downs of mediating, build expertise, and gain support from each other.

If, for example, you were interested in working in a profession with people who are likely to come into disputes and conflict – social services, for example, or youth work, law, the police and prison service, or Human Resources – then the training and experience volunteering with an organization like the Brighton and Hove Mediator Service could be invaluable.

Another example of an organization that provides free training is Missing Maps www.missingmaps.org/. Missing Maps is a project in which you can help to map areas where humanitarian organizations are trying to meet the needs of vulnerable people. Missing Maps says that it's no problem if you've not mapped before – it doesn't take long to learn; you just need to visit the beginners section on their website to find out how.

Volunteer centres can let you know what voluntary work is available in your area and put you in touch with local organizations. You can also discuss with them what you're interested in and get advice. Find out about volunteering opportunities near you by going to www.ncvo.org.uk/ or https://do-it.org/.

Look in the back of this book for information about organizations with opportunities to work as a volunteer in sectors such as environmental and wildlife, animal welfare, social work, or children and young people.

Most voluntary opportunities are advertised on an organization's website. However, if you have a particular organization and/or volunteer role in mind but you can't see any openings, do get in touch anyway. Explain what your interest is and why you want to volunteer with them. Look for a specific person to contact and address your email directly to them.

The amount of time you can devote to voluntary work depends, of course, on work, study, and/or family commitments. Be realistic about how much time you can commit. But whether it's a couple of hours a week, a few days a month, or part of a holiday, whatever you're interested in, there's bound to be a volunteer opportunity out there for you that will give you the opportunity to find out more about a profession or job sector.

Take a Course

Informational interviews, work shadowing, and volunteering are all ways to find out more about a job, work, or career you might be interested in. Another way is to do a short course or workshop, to explore what's available and convenient for you.

Even if you can't attend a course or workshop in person, there's a wide variety of online courses that will enable you to get an insight, gain knowledge, and perhaps learn a specific skill related to the job, the work, or career you're interested in. If, for example, you are interested in working in publishing, doing an accredited proofreading, copyediting, or indexing course would give you an insight, experience, and skills that, one way or another, will be helpful.

- Find Courses www.findcourses.co.uk/ allows you to search and compare a wide range of courses.
- Udemy www.udemy.com/ online learning platform is aimed at professional adults and students.
- Corsera www.coursera.org/ offers online courses, specializations, and degrees.
- Lynda www.lynda.com/ offers video courses taught by industry experts in software, creative, and business skills.
- The Open University (OU) www.open.ac.uk/ offers more than degrees. Their Short Courses programme is for those people who want to study entirely online for personal interest or professional development.
- Open University Access courses are for you if you want to improve your confidence with study, especially if you haven't studied for a while. And the OU's Microcredential courses are useful if you want to build professional skills and earn transferable academic credit.
- Future Learn www.futurelearn.com/ allows you to learn online with world-class universities and industry experts. Their courses are for people who want to develop their career, learn a new skill, or pursue a specific interest or hobby. A wide range of Future Learn's courses are free!

- LinkedIn Learning www.linkedin.com/learning/ allows you to learn business, creative, and technology skills to achieve your personal and professional goals. Again, many are free!

In a nutshell

- Informational interviews, work shadowing, and volunteering are all ways to find out more about a job, work, or career you might be interested in.
- To find people you could talk to or work shadow, start with your own informal network: friends, family, etc.
- Outside of your informal network, there are a number of ways you can find people and make contact with them. Google, LinkedIn, Facebook, Instagram, and Twitter are all helpful resources.
- Networking events, professional associations, Chambers of Commerce, training courses, and conferences are all good places to meet people in the profession or career that appeals to you. So are jobs and careers fairs.
- Once you start connecting with people, you'll be building a network of contacts that may be useful in future. People who are willing to take the time to help you are people you need to keep as contacts. So if, having talked with them or shadowed them, you're still interested in the role or profession, do ask to connect with them on LinkedIn.

- Voluntary work can help you to find out more about a specific industry or profession. You can get free training, gain practical experience, learn new skills, meet people, make new contacts, and get a reference for future job applications.
- As well as informational interviews, work shadowing, and volunteering, there's a wide variety of courses available to you that will enable you to get an insight, gain knowledge, and perhaps learn a specific skill related to the job, work, or career you're interested in.

6
Internships, Returnships, and Apprenticeships

If opportunity doesn't knock, build a door.

Milton Berle

Once you've narrowed down your ideas and identified a role, a job or career you're interested in, you'll want to know how to get into the job, profession, or career. In this chapter, you can read about internships, returnships, and apprenticeships.

Internships and Returnships

Internships provide practical work experience for someone new to an occupation or profession. They are typically undertaken by students and graduates.

Depending on the sector and employer, internships can be for a few weeks or up to a year. Student internships tend to be shorter in length than graduate ones; student internships usually last the length of a university summer break – two or three months – long enough for you to get a taste of the job and gain knowledge and skills. Graduate internships are longer – they usually take place for up to a year.

Getting an internship can be as competitive a process as getting a permanent job. You might need to apply many months in advance. Some organizations will have a specific deadline, so make sure you know when that is, for any internship that interests you.

Rate My Placement Work Ready Virtual Experience http://www.ratemyplacement.co.uk/jobs/19954/ratemy placement/work-ready-virtual-experience enables you to develop work-readiness skills to help you find work experience. InsideSherpa www.insidesherpa.com/ offers virtual work experience programmes in which top companies teach students the skills they hire for before they hire you.

To find internships, search for graduate internships at www.prospects.ac.uk/ and take a look at their employer profiles to see what opportunities different organizations offer. Bright Network www.brightnetwork.co.uk/ and www.ratemyplacement.co.uk/ also list internship opportunities.

Large companies usually advertise their internship and work placement schemes but small and medium-sized enterprises (SMEs) may take speculative applications. So do search out smaller organizations in your area of interest that you could approach for an internship or work experience.

Call the company beforehand to find out who to send your enquiries to and their contact details. Addressing your application to a specific person will show that you're genuinely interested in that company and not that you're simply blanket emailing several different companies. If all you can find is the company email address, send an initial email or phone asking for the contact details of the person you should email to make an enquiry about a work placement or internship.

You'll need to explain:

- Who you are and what you're currently doing or studying.
- Why you would like to do an internship/work experience.
- What knowledge and experience you already have of the profession/industry and why that profession/industry interests you.
- Any skills, qualifications, and other work experience or relevant training you have that would relate to the work experience requested.
- Why you want to work for that particular company: explain your interest in the company and say how this relates to what attracts you, in relation to a future career. If you want an organization to be interested in you, you need to demonstrate knowledge of the company and your genuine interest in working for them.
- How you think that you could benefit from the internship.
- What you can offer the company.

Ask whether, if the type of experience you're looking for isn't possible, there would be something similar. Attach your CV. If your request doesn't receive a response within one or two weeks, follow it up with an email or phone call.

Whether you organize your own internship or you're offered one through an internship scheme, if you are performing the role of a worker – if you work set hours and perform the same duties as paid members of staff – you can expect to receive at least the National Minimum Wage for your age range in the UK. You can find out more about pay for interns here: www.gov.uk/employment-rights-for-interns.

The Institute of Student Employers Annual Recruitment Survey 2018 found that employers rehired an average of 52% of their interns and 43% of their summer placement students. So, although employers often recruit employees from their interns, clearly not all internships lead to a job. While some people do an internship to develop their skills, knowledge, and experience, others hope the internship will lead to a permanent position. If this is your hope, do check how likely it is with a specific employer before applying.

Returnships

Routes back into work for older people are now becoming more common. First launched by the investment bank Goldman Sachs in the US in 2008, returnships are internships which act as a bridge to senior roles for experienced professionals who have taken an extended career break. They are paid roles that last a few months and often lead to a permanent role.

Returnships allow the 'returner' to update skills, knowledge, and experience in their previous sector or role or they might move into a new sector. A returnship programme is of benefit to employers because it gives them access to experienced and skilled workers.

Starting an internship at the age of 48

It's not just young people and students who can do an internship. Katherine Forster was 48 when she was accepted as an intern on *The Spectator*, a weekly British magazine on politics, culture, and current affairs. After A-levels, Katherine studied for a degree in English. She then trained as an actor, before spending 15 years bringing up her three sons.

In an article published in *The Times* in March 2020, Katherine described how, having been out of the workforce for so long, she assumed that getting any job would be hard. 'Dreaming of starting in a wildly competitive profession at my age was daft and deluded. I was too old. It was too late.'

Although Katherine had no contacts in the media and no journalistic qualifications, when *The Spectator* tweeted that they were looking for interns Katherine

---

nevertheless applied. 'I knew instantly this was my big chance. I probably wouldn't get it, but maybe, just maybe, I might.'

The Spectator's internship scheme had a no-CV policy: it didn't matter if you were 16 or 60, they selected on merit. Katherine had to send a 200-word blog, provide three suggestions for articles, and fact-check an article. She also made a three-minute audio file analyzing a Prime Minister's Question Time. Out of 150 applications, only a dozen got through.

In the *Times* article, Katherine wrote: 'So what if interns were usually less than half my age? I was happy to start at the bottom and didn't much care what people thought. I got the *Spectator* internship and they asked me to write about it for their pages. "Starting Again at 48" was one of *The Spectator*'s most-read articles of 2017.'

Katherine is now a journalist at *The Sunday Times* and she regularly appears on the BBC and Sky as a commentator.

Returnships originally focused companies on helping older workers, mainly women, return to work after career breaks for childcare responsibilities. But men do this too. Both women and men may have taken time out for childcare, to care for a family member, travel, or study. Advertising a returnship for female candidates is discrimination on the grounds of gender, as is having a policy to only select women to interview for a role.

Women Returners www.womenreturners.com/ works with employers and career returners to enable professional women and men to return to work after an extended career break. So does Runneth London www.runnethlondon.com/returnships/. The Return Hub www.thereturnhub.com/ also places professionals who want to relaunch after a career break or transfer their careers with employers in the financial services sector.

Apprenticeships

According to the Department for Education, 90% of apprentices stay employed after completing an apprenticeship. Apprenticeships combine practical training in a job with study. As an apprentice, you are a paid employee with a contract of employment and holiday entitlement.

Apprenticeships are for anyone; whether you're looking to start a job or career after leaving education, or you want to change career direction, you're never too old to do an apprenticeship. There's equal access to apprenticeships and so your age shouldn't affect whether you'll get onto an apprenticeship.

As an apprentice, your employer will pay you a salary and support you in your training. You'll be paid for the hours you work and the hours you do the training – which could be up to degree level.

Some employers offer their current members of staff an apprenticeship – anything from management to engineering qualifications – to help them develop and progress. In fact, if you're experienced in a particular work role, an apprenticeship at degree level could be the next step for you, so do find out more about what's available and talk to your employer about supporting you through an apprenticeship.

From accounting, digital marketing, and hairdressing to dental healthcare and textile manufacturing, there's a wide variety of apprenticeships available. Apprenticeships take one to five years to complete, depending on their level; there's a range of levels from level 2 – which is equivalent to GCSE study – to levels 6 and 7 – degree-level study. A degree apprenticeship is a relatively new type of apprenticeship, which leads to a full university degree, but without the tuition fees.

- The government website is a good starting point for researching apprenticeships, from application criteria to pay and conditions: www.gov.uk/apprenticeships-guide
- You can find apprenticeships in your area by going to www.gov.uk/apply-apprenticeship
- The website 'Get My First Job' has information too: www.getmyfirstjob.co.uk. So does Amazing Apprenticeships https://amazingapprenticeships.com/
- For degree-level apprenticeships go to www.ucas .com/understanding-apprenticeships
- Which? University has teamed up with the National Apprenticeship Service to create a downloadable

guide to higher and degree apprenticeships: www
.ucas.com/file/301156/download?token=Ikr35v3v
- White Hat – https://whitehat.org.uk/ matches non-
graduate talent with apprenticeship opportunities
with UK companies.

Voluntary Work

In the last chapter, you will have read that voluntary
work can help you find out more about a specific industry or profession. You can get free training, gain practical
experience, learn new skills, meet new people, and make
new contacts. There's more information about voluntary
organizations on pages 157–160.

Remember, too, that working as a volunteer for an organization could very well lead to a paid job within that
organization. For many employers, it's not so important
where you developed the skills, knowledge, or experience, it's the fact that you *do have* skills, knowledge, and
experience and you were proactive in getting them. It can
help you to stand out from others. It shows you have initiative and are obviously keen on the role, profession, or
industry.

In a nutshell

- Internships provide practical work experience for someone new to an occupation or
profession.

- Getting an internship can be a competitive process and you will probably need to apply months in advance.
- Large companies usually advertise their internship and work placement schemes but small and medium-sized enterprises (SMEs) may take speculative applications. Search out smaller organizations in your area of interest that you could approach for an internship or work experience.
- Returnships allow the 'returner' to update skills, knowledge, and experience in their previous sector or role or they might move into a new sector. Returnships are paid roles that last a few months and often lead to a permanent role.
- Apprenticeships combine practical training in a job with study.
- Apprenticeships are for anyone, whether you're looking to start a job or career after leaving education, or you want to change career direction. There's equal access to apprenticeships so your age shouldn't be an issue.
- As an apprentice, your employer will pay you a salary and support you in your training. You'll be paid for the hours you work and the hours you do the training – which could be up to degree level.
- Working as a volunteer for an organization can give you the skills, knowledge, and experience that could very well lead to a paid job within that organization.

7

Portfolio Careers and Side Hustles

For as soon as the distribution of labour comes into being, each man has a particular, exclusive sphere of activity, which is forced upon him and from which he cannot escape. He is a hunter, a fisherman, a herdsman, or a critical critic, and must remain so if he does not want to lose his means of livelihood; while in communist society, where nobody has one exclusive sphere of activity but each can become accomplished in any branch he wishes, society regulates the general production and thus makes it possible for me to do one thing today and another tomorrow, to hunt in the morning, fish in the afternoon, rear cattle in the evening, criticise after dinner, just as I have a mind, without ever becoming hunter, fisherman, herdsman or critic.

Karl Marx, *The German Ideology* 1846

Have you got more than one idea for a career or job that interests you? Are you struggling with which line of work to pursue? Perhaps you can't decide between work that offers stability and security or a job that gives you autonomy and flexibility. Maybe you have more than one interest and you can't choose which one to follow; you're trained as an upholsterer – it's something you enjoy doing – but you're also a qualified canoe instructor, for example. Or you want to work full-time hours but not in the same job in the same place every day; perhaps being in an office all day every day is too much, you need time to work outdoors, too. It could be that a particular job you're interested in is only available as a part-time position but won't pay enough to meet your needs. Or maybe you can't decide between working for an employer and working freelance.

What if you didn't have to decide? If any of the scenarios above sounds like a dilemma you have, then a portfolio career could be right for you.

A portfolio career simply involves dividing your time and skills between two or more part-time jobs; you have a portfolio of skills and interests that you carry from one job, or place of work, to another. Each job might use the same skills, be in a similar field, or they could be completely unrelated. The flexibility, autonomy, and variety that come with a portfolio career can be an attractive prospect to anyone who is more of a 'wide achiever' than a 'high achiever'.

There are a number of different shapes and forms a portfolio career can take: you could have one job as an employee and another self-employed. Or you might have two self-employed roles or two part-time jobs working as an employee.

If you have both an employed role and a self-employed role, you will probably have one primary source of income – the 'anchor' – working for an employer as an employee and other work running your own business, freelancing, working as a contractor, or as a consultancy. You could be working three days a week for an employer and the rest of the time you spend running your own business. You might, for example, be both self-employed as piano teacher and employed as a driving instructor. You could be employed as a teaching assistant in a primary school and be self-employed teaching a foreign language online. Or you might be employed in marketing, freelance as a copywriter, *and* run an online coaching business.

Employed and self-employed

Jesse works part-time as a receptionist at a photography studio, alongside being a freelance artist, designing and making his own greetings cards.

After completing a graphic design degree, Jesse started a temping job at the photography studio. Initially, he did it to financially support some freelance graphic design work he was doing, but he soon realized how much he enjoyed the work and that he could quite happily do both.

Doing this – working in an employed role *and* in a self-employed role – has given Jesse the financial security to do the creative work he wants to do, without having to worry too much about how much money the greetings card business makes. Several of Jesse's fellow students from his graphic design degree course have been doing the same since they graduated; they combine their creative self-employed work, where income isn't high, with more steady work.

Maybe, though, you don't want to be self-employed or work on a freelance basis. Having two jobs working for two different employers can still give you the variety you might be looking for. You could, for example, be employed working as a carer in a care home, and also work for an employer in a coffee shop. Or you might be employed by an office manager for a small architectural practice three days a week and for the other two days a week, you might be employed as an architectural research assistant for a different, much larger organization that looks at the effects of climate change on our cities and environment.

Two different jobs

Lily works as a gardener for a landscaping company two days a week and for the other three days she works in the finance department of a charity that promotes gardening to bring about positive changes in the lives of people living in deprived areas of cities and large towns.

'I've been working for the charity for two years, and the gardening I only started six months ago. I love it! I've just signed up for a series of Saturday courses in order to get some qualifications in horticulture.'

Lily's two employed roles are related, but different, giving her the opportunity to work in an office *and* outdoors.

Having a portfolio career means that you have variety in your week. And if one job – whether employed or self-employed – dries up or slows down, the other job or jobs are still there to support you.

A portfolio career can also be rebalanced whenever circumstances present themselves. A life change – for example, becoming a parent and working part-time from home on one of your jobs – can give you the flexible hours you need. When, for example, my friends Bill and Ron's children were small, Ron continued in her work as an orthopaedic surgeon. Her journalist husband Bill was at home with the children and taught journalism part-time at a local college. (When their children grew up, Bill changed direction completely and, together with a friend, he opened a restaurant.)

However, juggling two or more jobs isn't without its challenges, especially if one or more of those roles is self-employed. You'll need to be well organized, able to mentally compartmentalize, and have an open, flexible approach to manage this way of working.

Side Hustle or Side Project

If you already have a steady full-time job, one way to create a portfolio career – especially one that includes a self-employed role – is to start with a side hustle. A side hustle – or side project – is work you do in the evenings and at weekends, alongside your current job.

There are a number of advantages to starting a side project, the main advantage being that you can do it without having to give up your job as an employee; you can build up a self-employed income, while you still have the safety and security of your day job. Income from your job as an employee provides security, while the side hustle gives you the opportunity to experiment; to be innovative and take some risks in order to develop a potential job, business, or career you are interested in.

Annie, for example, was working as a tutor for a mental health organization, delivering courses and workshops on well-being. She took an online course in journalism and then started a side project as a freelance writer, writing articles on well-being and mental health.

Parveen was employed as a life guard at her local swimming pool. She loved textiles and fashion and started selling vintage clothing on Etsy, the e-commerce website.

She developed this into altering vintage pieces to fit and hand-embroidering vintage jeans. She hopes to turn her business into a full-time job and eventually run a shop in her nearby town.

Michael worked at an independent record store during the day and began putting on bands in pubs in the large town where he lived two evenings a week.

A side hustle can also create career-changing opportunities you may not have been able to access in your full-time job; you can build the skills, knowledge, contacts, and experience you need to change industry or profession. But if, for one reason or another, it doesn't succeed, it's been a relatively safe, risk-free way to find out.

Before you start a side project, you'll need to check the terms of your employment contract to see if there are any clauses that might affect your freedom to run your own business on the side. If there are no restrictions you can go ahead with your idea.

Look for a low-key way you can offer your product or service in order to get started. With even one client, or a few sales, you'll get an idea of what it's like to manage a portfolio career. Don't obsess about getting everything perfect before you launch; aiming for perfection will bog you down and prevent you from ever getting started. It's called a 'side hustle' for a reason! You have to hustle, to move forward with speed and deliberation, to push your way through.

As your business develops, you'll be able to develop your skills and knowledge, take on more clients or customers, and establish yourself more firmly in your second area.

Building a side hustle to profitability with a limited amount of time outside of your day job will though, take time, energy, and effort. You may need to figure out some of the activities that take up unnecessary time in your life. Then see which ones you can streamline or get rid of. This way, you can have more time to spend on your side hustle.

However, pursuing a side hustle that excites you and that you're good at could make all the difference in terms of how you feel about the time and energy you put into it.

It may be that freelancing or starting a business is not what you're aiming for. But you can still experiment with a portfolio career. Volunteering in the evenings and at weekends in an area or role that interests you (see pages 157–160) or taking on a very-part-time job can give you some experience of portfolio life, and help you gain skills and knowledge in the area of work that attracts you, meeting others and networking for the future.

Of course, the more success you achieve in your side project/business, the more you have to fit in! You might have to scale it back a bit if you want to keep it as part of a portfolio career. If, though, you are hoping to turn it into a full-time job but aren't quite ready to make the leap and leave your current full-time job as an employee, in order to have more hours to put into your side project – your fledgling business – you may be able to rearrange your hours in your employed job. There are a number of ways you could do this if the nature of your job allows for it. You could:

- Compress your hours; that is, work your usual hours, but in fewer days.
- Have a flexitime way of working; this allows you to fit your working hours around agreed core times.
- Work from home two or even five days of the week, cutting out commuting time and using it instead to put into your side project.

Flexible working might already be available within your company, so do find out what's on offer before making a more formal request. In the UK, after 26 weeks of continuous service, you have the right to make a formal request. Your request is more likely to be approved if you've taken into account their needs as well as your own. Explain how the changes will work for both you and your employer. This shows that you've put some real thought into the change, and can justify why it's a good idea. If your proposed changes could affect the business negatively, then your employer may have a good reason to say no. So do address the possible difficulties, and suggest realistic ways to overcome them. You can find out what you need to do by going to www.acas.org.uk/flexibleworking or Citizens Advice www.citizensadvice.org.uk and looking for their page on flexible working.

If you've tested out a new idea, you want to make it your full-time role, and all the signs are promising, you may want to take the plunge, leave your employed job, and make your side hustle your new full-time job.

From side hustle to a full-time business

Shona started off with a side hustle and then took a considered jump.

'I started Pineapple Polly Creative as a side project whilst working full time. I always knew I wanted to do something creative and my day job as a business analyst just wasn't giving me the opportunity to bring out that side of me. I started off doing wedding invitations, selling them on Etsy. I did the side hustle thing for a couple of years during which time I went on some courses – to help me learn about marketing my product and also to manage my finances. I expanded the range of wedding-related stationery – place cards, seating plans, Thank You cards, etc and things took off from there.'

A good way to find out more about the pros and cons of portfolio life is to ask people who are already doing it. There are a number of ways of running a portfolio career and different people make it work for them in different ways. Arrange a couple of 'informational interviews' (see Chapter 5) Ask portfolio careerists why they've chosen their particular combination of employment and/or self-employment; how they manage their time, what the difficulties are, what you might need to know before you start and as you go along.

The more ways of portfolio working you learn about, the better informed you'll be and better able to establish and develop a setup that suits you.

In a nutshell

- A portfolio career involves dividing your time and skills between two or more part-time jobs; you have a portfolio of skills and interests that you carry from one job, or place of work, to another. Each job might use the same skills, be in a similar field, or they could be completely unrelated.
- You might have one job working as an employee and another self-employed. Or you might have two self-employed roles or two part-time jobs working as an employee.
- Having a portfolio career means that you have variety in your week. And, if one job dries up or slows down, the other job or jobs are still there to support you. A portfolio career can also be rebalanced whenever circumstances in your life present themselves.
- You'll need to be well organized, able to mentally compartmentalize, and have an open, flexible approach to manage a portfolio career.
- If you already have a steady full-time job, one way to create a portfolio career – especially one that includes a self-employed role – is to start with a side hustle.

- The main benefit of a side hustle is that income from your job as an employee provides security, while the side hustle gives you the opportunity to experiment; to be innovative and take some risks in order to develop a potential job, business, or career you are interested in.
- A side hustle can also create career-changing opportunities; you can build the skills, knowledge, contacts, and experience you need to change industry or profession. But if, for one reason or another, it doesn't succeed, it's been a relatively safe, risk-free way to find out.
- Look for a low-key way to get started with your side hustle. Don't obsess about getting everything perfect first; aiming for perfection will bog you down and prevent you getting started.
- If self-employment isn't for you, voluntary work or taking on a very-part-time job can give you some experience of portfolio life, and help you gain skills and knowledge in the area of work that interests you, meeting others and networking for the future.
- If you're not quite ready to turn your side hustle into a full-time job – you may be able to rearrange your hours in your employed job.
- To find out more about the pros and cons of portfolio life, talk to people who are already doing it.

8

Being Stuck in a Job, Quitting a Job, and Managing Unemployment

It's not what you achieve, it's what you overcome. That's what defines your career.

Carlton Fisk

Make the Best of a Bad Job; Make Your Job Work for You

What if you're in a job, doing work or you're in a career that you don't like – it's not for you? Perhaps it's meaningless, boring, and uninteresting. Maybe it doesn't reflect your values, allow you to use or develop your knowledge and skills, but right now, much as you'd like to, for whatever reason, you can't quit. Is there anything you can do to help make your time at work more bearable? The answer is yes; whether it's a full-time job, a part-time job, an internship, or an apprenticeship there *are* steps you can take to improve your situation.

Think positive. First, know that that no matter how bad things are, you can always make things worse. Beware of confirmation bias. Confirmation bias happens when you look for evidence to support and confirm what you've already decided is true: that your job is crap. With confirmation bias it's easy to give too much weight to negative aspects and too little to the positive elements of a situation.

The more you dislike your job or aspects of your job, the more you'll find evidence to back up your dislike. 'See? They're making me do all the name tags for the event. It's ridiculous. There's more important things I could be doing.' Your life becomes a day-to-day exercise in proving yourself right.

Whatever the problem is, by focusing so intently on it you're choosing to make yourself unhappy.

Be aware that when negative thoughts take control, they limit your ability to see opportunities for positive action. Stop with the negativity and instead, if you can't leave, look for the positive aspects of your job. Is your job close to home and so you have a short journey to work? Is your commute a long one but you get to listen to the radio or podcasts in the car, or you get to read, listen to, or watch something on a tablet on the train? Your boss might be awful but maybe your colleagues are great?

If you *are* truly stuck there, you have to find a way to make the best of it. The way to do that is not only to focus on the positive, but also to focus on what you *can* control. Instead of making yourself miserable railing against the things you can't change, look to see what you *can* change.

As Reinhold Niebuhr's 'Serenity Prayer' says, 'God grant me the serenity to accept the things I cannot change; courage to change the things I can; and wisdom to know the difference.'

Negotiate your hours. Perhaps you have the sort of job where you could negotiate some time working from home? Or maybe you could reduce your hours? If you think you could manage on less money, asking to reduce your hours can be an effective way to spend less time working somewhere that you're unhappy and give you more time and space to pursue interests outside of your job. You'll feel less defined by the job; it won't be such a dominant part of your life. Working fewer hours could also free you up to start a side hustle and/or learn new skills.

Create your own meaning and purpose; learn new skills. Whether or not you can work from home or reduce your hours, if you're currently stuck in a job you don't like, aim to take charge of your own professional and personal development. There are a number of ways you can do this.

One approach is to set yourself a challenge. Choose an aspect of your job that is particularly onerous – difficult, boring, irritating, etc. Then set yourself a challenge to make it less difficult, boring, irritating, etc. Maybe, for example, you have a job where you often have to listen to other people's complaints. Take it on as a challenge; make it your goal to become really good at managing and resolving customer complaints.

Is there something missing – something that relates to your values – that you could bring into your work? Perhaps you'd like your work to have more social impact? Here's what Sean did: 'I got in touch with local charities and community groups to discuss ways that our company could collaborate with them to provide services to help a client group that was completely different from our main client group. Not only did I start enjoying my job more, it also gave me the kind of experience I wanted for the work I knew that I really wanted to do in future.'

Maybe you could take the lead on initiating changes and improvements at work: a more comfortable working environment, or more efficient methods and procedures, or a flexible working policy? If you're feeling unfulfilled and unhappy, finding the motivation to take the lead on something probably isn't going to feel like the obvious and enjoyable thing to do. But it does provide you with some meaning and purpose in your working week and it'll give you an extra skill for your next job.

In fact, just because you're not able to leave your job right now doesn't mean you can't start working towards the next one. What would you like to do in your next job – is there a skill you'll need that you can develop in this job?

Think about developing a skill or an aspect of your job that you're already quite good at or enjoy doing. If, for example, the one part of your job you enjoy is giving presentations to colleagues or potential clients, then you could further develop your presentation skills. You could take a free online course. Watch a few TED talks – www.ted.com – pick out the best presenters, decide what's good about their presentation skills, and aim to do the same.

Whatever aspect of your job you like, do whatever you need to do to get really, really good at it and make it as much a part of your job as you can.

Find out about training already offered at work. Find out, too, about other training, courses, and workshops relevant to your job and ask if you can attend or if an outside trainer can come in and deliver training to you and other colleagues.

You have to decide for yourself that you're going to make your work meaningful. But if you can't develop new skills and challenges related to your work, then look for other ways you can learn new skills.

Alex was saving to travel in South America for six months. He had a night job stacking shelves at a supermarket. The work was boring, dull, and repetitive. But he downloaded a language course so that while he was stacking shelves, he learnt Spanish.

You can learn new skills – retrain, study – in your lunchtime, on your commute, in the evenings, or at weekends. Izzy decided to learn how to code. 'I knew it would be a useful skill, something that I could do freelance in future and it would enable me to work on my own terms. I signed up to two courses: one online and one in person at a local adult learning centre. I've enjoyed learning how to code. Now, in all the boring meetings at work, instead of getting wound up thinking what a waste of time it all is, I'm planning my next website or solving a programming problem in my head. Having something different and enjoyable to focus on has helped me to be happier.'

As well as doing a course to learn new skills and knowledge, finding a voluntary role related to something you might like to do as a job in future can help you to find out more about a specific industry or profession. You can get free training, gain practical experience, learn new skills, meet people, make new contacts, and get a reference for a future job applications. There's lots of information about voluntary work opportunities on pages 157–160.

If you feel you're made for better things, then you probably are! It's very likely that there is another direction waiting for you, one that will bring more reward, recognition, and satisfaction to your life. You just need to get out there and make it happen!

Knowing When it's Time to Quit

But what if it's not just that you feel that the 'real you' can't come out in this job – it's meaningless, boring, uninteresting, and doesn't allow you to use or develop your skills or knowledge. What if it's more than that? How do you know when you should give your job a second chance, or when it really is time to quit?

Perhaps your job is stressful. You feel overworked and unappreciated, or you hate your boss and don't like your colleagues, clients, or customers.

Maybe the work environment is negative. You don't feel psychologically safe; you don't feel confident and comfortable enough at work to voice your opinion, share your thoughts, and speak up for yourself. Perhaps you're being bullied or there's a culture of bullying at your workplace. It could be that you don't believe in what the company you work for is putting out in the world, or how they're doing it; you think that what your employer is doing is unnecessary or actually unsafe.

Maybe your work–life balance is completely out of sync; you're working too many hours – and even when you're not working, you're thinking about it – so that you have little in the way of time or energy for family, friends, or outside interests.

Do you dread going to work and you're unhappy when you're there?

It could be that workplace stress is taking a toll on your physical or mental health. You're constantly stressed: overwhelmed and worried; unable to concentrate; feeling irritable, impatient, and aggressive. You suffer from muscle tension, headaches, and/or digestive issues. Perhaps you suffer from sleep problems. Maybe you're resorting to drink or drugs each night to get over yet another bad day at work?

No job is worth sacrificing your well-being, physical, and mental health. You *must* do something!

Stress: Know your rights

The UK's Health and Safety Executive say that 'if you are feeling signs of stress at work, it is important to talk to someone, for example your manager. If you talk to them as soon as possible, it will give them the chance to help and stop the situation getting worse.'

In the UK, your employer has a legal duty to assess the risks to your health from stress at work and share the results of any risk assessment with you. So, do find out if a risk assessment has been done and also see what policies are in place at work to deal with stress.

If you feel unable to talk to your manager you can talk to one of the following, for advice and guidance:

- Your trade union representative
- ACAS acas.org.uk/
- An employee representative
- Your HR department
- An employee assistance programme/counselling service if your company has these, or
- Your GP.

Do not tolerate bullying and harassment

Bullying happens when one person is being persistently badgering, dominating, or intimidating; continually criticizing, insulting, or humiliating another person. Bullying, as defined by Acas, is 'offensive, intimidating, malicious or insulting behaviour, an abuse or misuse of power through means that undermine, humiliate, denigrate or injure the recipient'. Bullying can happen to anyone.

By law, it amounts to harassment when bullying or unwanted behaviour is about any of the following (known as 'protected characteristics'): a person's age, their race, disability, gender reassignment, pregnancy and maternity, religion or belief, sex or their sexual orientation.

Harassment, as defined in the Equality Act 2010, is 'unwanted conduct related to a relevant protected characteristic, which has the purpose or effect of violating an individual's dignity or creating an intimidating, hostile, degrading, humiliating or offensive environment for that individual'.

If you're being bullied then you may well feel very upset; anxious and frightened, ashamed or embarrassed. You may feel angry and frustrated. You mustn't try and pacify or ingratiate yourself with the bully, but you *must* do something. The bully will not go away. Staying silent and telling no one will only isolate you while at the same time empowering the bully, so you must get some help and support. Don't suffer in silence; there *is* help out there.

To start with, find out if your employer has a policy on bullying. The policy should outline how to address the problem and what the grievance procedure is. If you're not ready or feel unable to talk to someone at work about it, Acas have advice on their website acas.org.uk (search for Bullying and Harassment at Work – a Guide for Employees). Acas also have a helpline that can provide you with advice on what to do if you're being bullied at work; you can find the phone number on their website. Citizens Advice citizensadvice.org.uk can also provide information and advice. Go to their website and search for 'If you're being harassed or bullied at work'.

If you're being bullied and nothing changes for the better, or you do not feel as if you can take action, you may decide that leaving your job is the best option for your well-being and mental health.

By leaving, you regain control; you take away the opportunity for the bully to behave like this towards you. Being bullied and trying to manage being bullied is highly stressful. Ask yourself what's most important? Is it that you don't want to let the bully 'win'? Is that the most important issue? Rather than thinking in terms of one of you winning or losing, it's far better to think about keeping yourself safe and sane. Yes, you might have to walk away from a good job and financial stability, but focus on the positive: you've left that person behind. Once you've left, you can put your energy into finding a new job instead of spending your energy trying to please, pacify, or avoid the bully.

If you do want to think in terms of who's won and who's lost – know that if you take control and walk away you have won. You *can* manage to find a new job or somewhere to live. What you can't manage is the bully. So refuse to allow your life to be wrecked and get out!

If, no matter what you've tried – your work environment is still negative, your work–life balance isn't getting better, the stress is too much, your physical or mental health is suffering – if things aren't improving, then it's time to get out.

Too often, instead of letting go and starting over, many of us simply stay in a career, a job, or a course we hate. Why, like so many people, might you be doing that?

Perhaps you can't see an alternative course of action. Often, it's difficult to walk away from a situation if you can't see what other path to take, especially if walking away could mean quite a big change in your life.

Maybe you feel you've made a commitment so now you should stick with it and put up with the difficulties. Perhaps you don't want to admit that you were wrong to have put up with a bad situation for so long. Anyway, you're so used to it, you might as well carry on.

You might be thinking about the sunk costs: the time, effort, or money you've already put in and that you can never get back. But sunk costs can fool you into sticking with something; you continue to put more time or effort into someone or something even though it's plainly not doing you any good.

Of course, you don't want to give up too easily, but refusing to let go of a job, career, or course of study that's making you miserable means you're allowing your past to dictate your present. Don't make the same mistake over and over. Know that strength shows not only in your ability to persist, but in your ability to start over – to let go of the past and begin again in the present.

Realize that, at the time, based on what you knew and how you felt, you did make the right choice. At the time, your decision was the right one. Now, though, the situation isn't right for you.

> If you can change your mind you can change your life.
>
> William James

Think positive. Instead of seeing yourself as having made a 'U Turn', see yourself as open-minded, flexible, and able to change and adapt according to new circumstances. See yourself as simply having made a new decision. You can always draw something good out. At the very least, you'll have learnt something about yourself. For example, you might now know that managing other people is not for you; that you're better off taking directions than giving them.

Have courage! Courage is the quality of mind or spirit that enables you to do something despite your fear and concerns. Courage is what makes you brave and helps you move forward. You may well feel concerned – worried and anxious – about telling someone else that you're going to leave the job, the career, or the course of study. That's OK. But rather than focus on how anxious you feel, think of how much better you'll feel for having done so. Having a few uncomfortable conversations is a small price to pay for freeing yourself from a situation that you've begun to resent and that is making you unhappy.

Quitting the Course

Quitting the course

A couple of years ago Dev got a place at university to study digital film production.

But by the end of the first term, he came to see that it wasn't right for him. He realized that, in three years' time, not only would he have a large debt, but even though he'd have a degree, he'd still have to start at the bottom of the film industry, as a runner. Dev knew he certainly didn't need a degree to be a runner. Rather than wait three years and have a £30,000 debt, Dev wanted to start as a runner straight away.

However, not only would he have to tell his parents and ask if he could move back home, but he'd already incurred that term's student loan, his parents had paid for that term's student accommodation, and he'd have to negotiate a way out of the student accommodation contract that committed him to being there until the end of the first year. He also knew that he'd have to really push to get work as a runner in the film business. None of this was going to be easy.

That was a year ago. Dev dealt with all the difficulties involved in leaving his university course. He's taken every running job that's come up, he works long hours – 14-hour days are not unusual. He's progressed from working as a runner and has recently had two jobs as a trainee cameraman. He's happy.

James realized that if he wanted to further his career in marketing, he would need to get some qualifications. With encouragement from his manager, he enrolled on a Diploma in Marketing course.

After the first module – which was three months long – James was struggling. 'Attending the class once a week was not a problem,' explains James. 'But there was a lot of homework each week. Trying to combine the studying and a full-time job wasn't easy but I persevered. I told myself I should keep going. Half way through the second module I was totally stressed out and I had little time for my friends or family.

Eventually I quit. What I had already learnt on the course had enabled me to get a new role at work anyway so I decided I didn't need the qualification. I certainly didn't need the stress, it was making me miserable.

Rather than feel bad about quitting, I saw it as "letting go" and I focused instead, on what I'd gained.

I applied the knowledge I had already gained from the course to my new job. And, I got my life back! Less stress and more time with friends and family.'

Like Dev and James, think about what you have to gain rather than what you have to lose by pulling out.

Whether you've struggled with a job, career, or course of study for a month, a year, or even half a lifetime, don't keep struggling on. Identify what you've gained from the experience – what positive things you've learnt about yourself – and what you will do differently now.

Be prepared to modify your goals. Your priorities and your goals may well change as time goes on, so adjust them to reflect new knowledge and experience. And if a specific goal no longer feels appropriate, then let it go. A few years ago, for example, I started a master's degree in Education with the Open University. Although it was interesting, after the first module, I changed my mind about continuing. I altered my goal – rather than pay to study, research, and write, I decided to find a way to be paid to research and write. And that was the first step towards writing my first book.

Managing Unemployment

Whether you've chosen to leave your job, been fired, laid off, forced to take redundancy or early retirement, or had freelance or contract work dry up, becoming unemployed can be one of life's most stressful experiences, affecting not just your finances, but also your relationships, confidence, and mental and emotional health.

Our jobs are often more than just the way we make a living. Even if you didn't love your job, work, or career, it can provide you with an identity – it shapes who you are and how others see you. Your job can provide you with social contact and support, providing purpose and structure to your days and weeks. Your work may have given you opportunities to use your skills and knowledge, and to acquire and develop new skills and knowledge.

Finding yourself out of work can take this all away from you, leaving you feeling hurt, angry, isolated, anxious, or depressed. You might experience a loss of confidence and self-esteem. Depending on the circumstances of your unemployment, you might feel let down by your employer, or blame yourself for something you think you should or shouldn't have done. You might now be feeling you have little or no control over the direction of your life; the stress, uncertainty, and worry can feel overwhelming. But no matter how bleak things seem right now, there is hope.

Acknowledge your sadness and anger. But don't get stuck. Tell yourself that you have every right to feel upset, anxious, or angry. Allow yourself to grieve; grief is a natural response to loss, and that includes the loss of a job. While we might each grieve in different ways, there are healthy and unhealthy ways to mourn the loss of your job. It can be easy to fall into drinking and/or smoking too much or bingeing on junk food for comfort. Don't try drowning or suppressing your feelings. Acknowledge your thoughts and emotions. It can help to put down in writing how you feel about leaving or losing your job and being unemployed, including things you wish you had – or hadn't – done.

Give yourself time. Take time to accept and adjust to your new reality. But avoid getting stuck, wallowing in the unfairness of it all, blaming yourself or others. Try to accept the situation. Acceptance simply means recognizing that you cannot change what has *already* happened. Once you can see that, you free yourself to get on with what you can do to move forward.

Think positive. Ask yourself what you've learnt – what helpful things – from this experience. Maybe unemployment has given you a chance to reflect on what you want out of life and rethink your priorities.

Challenge negative thoughts. If you start to think, 'I'll never get another job' write down evidence to the contrary: 'Of course I'll get another job. It will take time, but there *are* things I can do to make that happen.'

Don't put yourself down. Losing a job doesn't make you a loser; it means that you are part of an ever-changing workforce. Think of this as simply being 'in between jobs'. Think about how you would be kind to a friend going through unemployment. Then, be kind to yourself.

Get organized. Just because your last job came to an end doesn't mean you don't have a current job. Your current job is looking for a job. Put aside a couple of hours each day for your job search. This can include looking at ads and applying for jobs and courses, contacting people who might be able to help – to give information, ideas and advice, and more leads to contact.

Keep a regular daily routine. For anything you do towards a job search have a daily 'start' and 'end' time, with time out for breaks – meals, exercise, fresh air, meeting others, volunteer work etc. Following a set schedule will help you be more efficient and support your mental health and well-being.

Connect with other people. You might want to withdraw from other people. But other people – friends and family – can provide support. Talk to someone who is a good listener; someone who'll listen without judgement or offering unhelpful but well-meaning advice. Find those who *do* have good ideas and advice – you never know what opportunities will arise. Keep friends and past colleagues in the loop about your job search.

Find other ways to define yourself. Being unemployed doesn't have to define who you are; you can define yourself. Pursue activities that you enjoy and provide meaning and purpose. By pursuing hobbies, interests, and relationships, you can reaffirm that it's these things that define you as an individual, not your employment status. Take up a new interest. Join up with others to pursue an interest or hobby; take a look at meetup.com. Sign up for a course, learn a new skill or skills.

Volunteer. Helping others or supporting a cause that's important to you is an excellent way to maintain a sense of meaning and purpose in your life. A voluntary position usually comes with free training; you'll be able to learn new skills, meet people, make new contacts, and get a reference for a future job application. See pages 157–160 for more information about finding opportunities for voluntary work.

Focus on what you can control. Rather than spending time and energy worrying about situations that are out of your hands, keep your attention on what you can control, such as learning new skills, voluntary work, networking, etc.

Advice from the class of 2008

In June 2020, the world was experiencing a global pandemic. Twelve years earlier, in 2008, university graduates faced anxiety when the global financial crisis pitched much of the world into recession. Banks collapsed, businesses went under, and many, many people lost their jobs. Szu Ping Chan, a BBC business journalist on the BBC's news website asked three graduates from 2008 what advice they would give to those students graduating in the summer of 2020.

35-year-old Lindsay Cash explained that she took roles that helped her to build skills that she would use in the future. Lindsay's advice was that you need to accept that things don't always work out. 'But,' she says, 'you have to regroup and say: What do I need to do to move forward?'

Another 2008 graduate, Scott Wilson-Laing, explained that, as there was little in the way of graduate employment in his home town of Sunderland, he simply applied for anything and everything.

He spent a year working at a call centre, then a lighthouse for six months, and then a steel factory. 'For six years,' says Scott, 'I worked my way up from the production line to sales and operations, before moving to an IT company.'

Like Lindsay, Scott's advice is to stay as positive as you can and not to get stuck thinking about what didn't happen or work out. 'I thought my life was mapped out: go to university, get a job, stay for life, and get a nice retirement package at the end with a watch. And that's not the world we live in anymore. So be open to opportunities that you may not have planned for. Working in a call centre was where I learned the right way to treat and talk to staff. It's amazing the skills you pick up in jobs that you don't even realise.'

When 33-year-old Harriet Nicholson graduated from Oxford University in 2008 she was aiming for graduate schemes at consumer goods giants like Unilever and Reckitt Benckiser. She didn't get anywhere with this so she started applying for graduate schemes with other companies. After several months of applying unsuccessfully for jobs, Harriet moved back to her home town where she got a job as a medical receptionist.

'I felt embarrassed and had lost confidence', said Harriet. 'That job made me realise I wasn't as good as I thought I was. So many people I worked with could do my job better than me.' But then Harriet got an internship at Oxfam. 'This was instrumental because I made a lot of contacts and eventually did a master's degree in management. That got me on the career path I'm on now, which led to my current job at a digital consultancy. In retrospect, I held graduate schemes in really high esteem, which was actually a bit silly.... I didn't think about looking for an entry-level job to get a foot in the door there.'

Have an Open Mind and Be Persistent

When it comes to coping with unemployment and finding a new job or career, the way you think – your attitude and approach – makes all the difference. As far as possible, you'll need a positive mindset. This means that, on the one hand, you'll need persistence and determination, and on the other hand, an open mind: a willingness to be adaptable and flexible.

Whatever you want to do and however you've chosen to go about it, your plans don't need to be fixed. As you work towards whatever it is that you want to do you may need to adjust the steps you intend to take as a result of new knowledge and experience.

You will need to be flexible and open to the fact that problems might arise. Be prepared to change course in light of the unexpected. This doesn't mean that you're giving up on a good idea. It means that you're not limiting your chance of success by focusing on just one way to accomplish it. If you really want to achieve something, there's always a way. And most likely, there's more than one way.

You'll need to be persistent. Without persistence, not only do you achieve less than you're capable of, you don't even get to discover what you are capable of achieving. And you don't get the confidence that comes from pushing through and eventually succeeding. Persistence provides its own momentum. If you can just keep going, you'll eventually get results. And results motivate you to continue.

There's a difference, though, between being persistent and being stubborn. Being stubborn is being determined *not* to change your attitude or approach to something despite the evidence that things aren't working out.

But as Albert Einstein once said, 'Insanity is doing the same thing over and over again and expecting different results.' Being stubborn means you are less likely to step back so that you can get a broader perspective on what is and isn't happening and be more strategic. In contrast, when you're persistent, although you're determined to succeed, you can see when something is not working. You're flexible; you're able to adjust your plans and actions and are prepared to listen to suggestions, ideas, and advice. You're open to new ways of doing things so that you can keep moving forward, make things happen, and get things done.

Admittedly, the line between stubbornness and persistence is thin and it can be difficult to distinguish the two. But stubbornness leads to stagnation; it struggles on and it doesn't accept other possibilities, other ways of doing something. Persistence is a more uplifting experience; periods of difficulty are interspersed with small gains and measures of progress. These small gains inspire you and give you hope; you recognize and build on the small gains.

Think of a time when you've achieved something through persistence – passed your driving test, learnt to speak a language, master a musical instrument, or some other activity. No doubt it wasn't easy but you achieved it because you were persistent; when things became difficult, you found a way to overcome the challenges and you moved forward.

Having a positive outlook doesn't mean denying the challenges and difficulties of a situation. Rather, you acknowledge the difficulties and challenges and then, instead of letting them drag you down into a spiral of negative thinking, you move on to work out how you can now respond in positive, constructive ways. And you use the difficulties as learning experiences for the future.

In a nutshell

- If you're in a job, doing work, or you're in a career that you don't like, there *are* steps you can take to improve your situation.

- Think positive. Instead of making yourself miserable railing against the things you can't change, look to see what you *can* change; in particular, find a way to learn new skills or increase you knowledge.
- It's very likely that there *is* another direction waiting for you, one that will bring more rewards, recognition, and satisfaction to your life. You just need to get out there and make it happen!
- Too often, instead of letting go and starting over, many of us simply stay in a career, a job, or a course we hate.
- If, no matter what you've tried, your work environment is still negative, your work–life balance isn't getting better, the stress is too much, your physical or mental health is suffering – then it's time to get out.
- Think positive. Think about what you have to gain rather than what you have to lose by pulling out. You can always draw something good out. At the very least, you'll have learnt something about yourself.
- If you're unemployed, you might feel you have little or no control over the direction of your life. The stress, uncertainty, and worry can feel over-whelming. But there *is* hope.
- Give yourself time; time to accept and adjust to your new reality. But avoid getting stuck; wallowing in the unfairness of it all; blaming yourself or others.

- Think positive. Ask yourself what you have learned – what helpful things – from this experience.
- Get organized and keep a regular routine. Put aside a couple of hours each day for your job search: looking for work and applying for jobs and courses, connecting with others, learning new skills, doing voluntary work.
- When it comes to finding and getting a new job or career, the way you think – your attitude and approach – makes all the difference. As far as possible, you'll need a positive mindset, persistence and determination, an open mind, and a willingness to be adaptable and flexible.

Websites and Further Information

Job Roles and Profiles
- UCAS https://www.ucas.com/ucas/after-gcses/find-career-ideas/explore-jobs
- Prospects https://www.prospects.ac.uk/job-profiles/browse-a-to-z
- BBC Careers https://www.bbc.co.uk/bitesize/articles/zdqnxyc
- Career Hackers https://careerhacker.ai/explore-careers

Job Fairs
www.thejobfairs.co.uk

Work Shadowing
Viewvo https://viewvo.com

Voluntary Work in the UK
National Council for Voluntary Organisations (NVCO)
www.ncvo.org.uk
Do-it https://do-it.org
TimeBank https://timebank.org.uk
Vinspired https://vinspired.com
VolunteeringMatters https://volunteeringmatters.org.uk

Volunteer Now (Northern Ireland) www.volunteernow
.co.uk
Volunteer Scotland www.volunteerscotland.net
Volunteering Wales https://volunteering-wales.net

Volunteer Abroad

If you're interested in projects in other countries, there
are lots of opportunities to volunteer abroad.
Frontier https://frontier.ac.uk
Global Vision International (GVI) www.gvi.co.uk
International Volunteer HQ www.volunteerhq.org
Maximo Nivel https://maximonivel.com/volunteers
Kaya Responsible Travel www.kayavolunteer.com
Pod Volunteer www.podvolunteer.org
Shark & Marine Research Institute www.sharkcagedive
.com
Tru Experience Travel www.truexperiencetravel.co.uk
Voluntary Service Overseas (VSO) www.vsointernational
.org
Volunteer Abroad www.goabroad.com/volunteer-abroad
Workaway www.workaway.info

Environmental Volunteering

Wildlife Trust www.wildlifetrusts.org
Woodland Trust www.woodlandtrust.org.uk
Marine Conservation Society www.mcsuk.org
National Trust www.nationaltrust.org.uk

Volunteer Work with Animals

Blue Cross www.bluecross.org.uk/volunteer
The People's Dispensary for Sick Animals (PDSA) www
.pdsa.org.uk

The Royal Society for the Prevention of Cruelty to Animals (RSPCA) www.rspca.org.uk
Several UK charities help people with day-to-day living by providing contact with animals. These include:
Assistance Dogs UK www.dogsforgood.org
Pets as Therapy https://petsastherapy.org
Riding for the Disabled Association www.rda.org.uk/volunteer

Volunteer Work with Children and Young People
Girlguiding www.girlguiding.org.uk
Scouts Association www.scouts.org.uk
Princes Trust www.princes-trust.org.uk

Voluntary Work with Mental Health Organizations
- Mind www.mind.org.uk
- Sane www.sane.org.uk
- Stress Management Society www.stress.org.uk
- Anxiety UK www.anxietyuk.org.uk
- Samaritans www.samaritans.org
- Papyrus www.papyrus-uk.org

Voluntary Work in Museums
Both regional and national museums – all 2,500 of them in the UK – have volunteering opportunities, whether front-of-house or behind the scenes. Find one near you at www.museums.co.uk

Volunteering in Sports
Join In www.doit.life/join-in
Sport England www.sportengland.org

Medical Volunteering

St Johns Ambulance www.sja.org.uk
Red Cross www.redcross.org.uk
Festival Medical Services www.festival-medical.org/
get-involved

Courses, Training, and Study

- Find Courses www.findcourses.co.uk allows you to search and compare a wide range of courses
- Udemy www.udemy.com online learning platform is aimed at professional adults and students
- Corsera www.coursera.org offers online courses, specializations, and degrees
- Lynda www.lynda.com offers video courses taught by industry experts in software, creative, and business skills
- Open University (OU) www.open.ac.uk offers more than degrees. Their Short Courses programme is for those people who want to study entirely online for personal interest or professional development

OU's Access courses are for you if you want to improve your confidence for study, especially if you haven't studied for a while; and the OU's Microcredential courses if you want to build professional skills and earn transferable academic credit.

- Future Learn futurelearn.com allows you to learn online with world-class universities and industry experts. It is for people who want to develop their career, learn a new skill, or pursue a specific interest or hobby. A wide range of Future Learn's courses are free!

- LinkedIn Learning linkedin.com/learning Learn business, creative, and technology skills to achieve your personal and professional goals. Again, many are free!

Internships

Bright Network www.brightnetwork.co.uk

Prospects www.prospects.ac.uk

InsideSherpa www.insidesherpa.com offers free virtual internships provided by a variety of top companies. With Inside Sherpa's virtual work experience programmes, companies teach you the skills they hire for before they hire you

Rate My Placement www.ratemyplacement.co.uk

Rate My Placement Work Ready Virtual Experience http://www.ratemyplacement.co.uk/jobs/19954/ratemy placement/work-ready-virtual-experience enables you to develop work-readiness skills to help you find work experience

Career Change

Career Shifters https://www.careershifters.org help people who feel stuck in the wrong career find and move into more fulfilling work.

Returnships

Women Returners https://womenreturners.com

Runneth London https://runnethlondon.com/returnships

The Return Hub www.thereturnhub.com

Apprenticeships

gov.uk/apprenticeships-guide

gov.uk/apply-apprenticeship

White Hat https://whitehat.org.uk
Get My First Job www.getmyfirstjob.co.uk
Amazing Apprenticeships https://amazingapprentice
ships.com
UCAS www.ucas.com/understanding-apprenticeships

Creative Careers and Publishing
Creative Access https://creativeaccess.org.uk is an
organization supporting people from under-represented
backgrounds into creative careers
Get into Book Publishing getintobookpublishing.co.uk

CVs, Application Forms, Cover Letters, and Interviews
Reed www.reed.co.uk/career-advice
Prospects www.prospects.ac.uk/careers-advice/applying-
for-jobs
Indeed www.indeed.co.uk/career-advice
Monster www.monster.co.uk/career-advice

About the Author

Gill Hasson is a tutor, trainer, and writer. She has over 20 years' experience in the area of personal and career development, mental health and well-being.

Gill has worked as a tutor at both the University of Sussex and Sussex Careers Service, delivering careers courses to mature students. She now works as a freelance careers advisor and coach. gillhasson.co.uk

Gill delivers teaching and training for educational organizations, voluntary organizations, and the corporate and public sectors.

The courses and the people that she works with inspire the books that she writes. She has written more than 25 books on subjects such as emotional intelligence, mental health and well-being at work, mindfulness, positive thinking, and resilience.

To contact Gill, email her at gillhasson@btinternet.com

Index

Index

Index

Index

Index